A Taste of the West Country

A collection of original recipes created by
Taste of the West award-winning chefs and producers

wemakemagazines

A catalogue record for this book is available
from the British Library.

ISBN 978-0-9933352-2-8

Published by We Make Magazines Ltd
wemakemagazines.co.uk

Editor: Jennie Cooper
Sub-editor: Belinda Dillon
Designer: Jeff Cooper

Thanks to Jo Hall, Julie Hutchins and Jody Spencer.

Contents

Meat

James Kittow's Pen'n'Tinny Sausage, chickpea
and chorizo casserole   20

Quick Bowgie brunch using James Kittow's produce   24

Deli Farm Charcuterie Chorizo and Parmesan potato cakes   32

Parma ham-encrusted pork tenderloin with a Polgoon Cider
sauce and cider-poached apples, served with beans and peas   36

Cornish Duck Company duck breast with
sticky red cabbage, squash purée and poached pear   42

Crispy Cornish belly pork with St Ives Cider Apple Juice
jus and apple-infused mashed potatoes   48

Pan-fried Eversfield Organic Lamb loin chops with
crushed new potatoes, broad beans, garden peas and mint   72

Wild boar loin with Cox & Laflin Black Pudding
Scotch egg, roasted baby beets and sweet potato duo   80

Chunk of Devon's Ploughman's pasty   86

Wicked Wolf Gin-marinated Exmoor venison
with a gin, port and pomegranate sauce   90

Eggs Olivier, using Blackdown Hills West Country Eggs   106

Pan-roasted Somerset chicken supreme with baby carrots,
beetroot, green beans and sage and a Fussels Truffle Oil pesto   110

Slow-cooked Coombe Farm Organic Lamb with a ricotta,
fennel, lemon, spring onion and watercress salad   114

Pork, Honey & Mustard sausages from P&K Meats,
served with celeriac mash and apple sauce   118

Helen Browning's Organic Bacon, crab and herb
hotcakes, with poached eggs and crème fraîche   150

Vegetarian

Church House piccalilli served with
Quicke's Vintage Cheddar ploughman's   68

Beetroot tarte tatin with Symondsbury Produce Spiced
Beetroot & Orange Chutney, watercress salad and goats' cheese   124

Fish

Summer stew with pan-seared cod and
Deli Farm Charcuterie Cornish Coppa lardons — 30

Waterside Bistro fish soup served with rouille, Gruyère and croutons — 56

Exmouth mussels in a Crafty Cider, leek and bacon sauce — 64

Lyme Bay gilthead bream on crushed potatoes with
chorizo and a cucumber, tomato and red onion salsa — 100

Whole grilled Lyme Bay sole with Cornish
new potatoes, caper nut brown butter and brown shrimps — 104

Conker Spirit Dorset Dry Gin-cured sea trout
with a tonic gel and cucumber sorbet — 128

Mackerel tartare on toast with Wasabi Company wasabi — 136

Smoked trout with Watercress Company
Baby Leaf Salad and watercress dressing — 140

6X Gold ale-steamed mussels with whipped citrus tarragon
butter and chilli-crusted gluten-free 6X Gold beer bread — 144

Desserts

Cream tea cheesecake by Boscastle Farm Shop — 52

Cheesecake made with Lemon Meringue Fudge
from Roly's Fudge — 58

Bakewell cake filled with Clare's Preserves'
Pink Exmoor Gin Marmalade — 76

Edward's Chocolate Orange Fudge brownie — 94

Banana loaf made with Chocolate Orange Fudge
from Edward's Fudge Kitchen — 98

Almond, mint and raspberry roulade filled
with Lily's Produce Raspberry Jam — 132

Sauces

Tomato ketchup — 28

Foreword

The West Country is a bit of a trailblazer in the food world. Yes, we're blessed with green pastures, clean coastal waters and a landscape suitable for growing and farming a wide variety of produce. But these raw ingredients would be worthless if it wasn't for our talented, passionate growers, farmers, producers and chefs. We have plenty to celebrate, which is why we produce our ever-popular recipe book.

Now in its third year, *A Taste of the West Country* has once again brought together award-winning chefs and producers from Taste of the West to create this locally inspired keepsake. Each pair comes from Cornwall, Devon, Dorset, Somerset and Wiltshire, bringing you recipes using the finest local produce that is available all year round.

Using ingredients readily available around the region, these dishes have been created specifically for this book – straight from the chef's kitchen! You needn't be an accomplished cook to recreate them at home: all recipes have been compiled using easy-to-follow steps, and include some handy tips to help you along the way.

Not only will you impress your friends and family with these dishes, but you're also supporting our local food and drink industry. There's no better way to celebrate a true Taste of the West Country. We hope you enjoy cooking (and eating) our recipes.

John Sheaves
Chief Executive, Taste of the West

All recipes serve 4

Cornwall

James Kittow's Pen'n'Tinny Sausage, chickpea and chorizo casserole

Recipe by Richard du Pille, Head Chef,
Duchy of Cornwall Nursery, Lostwithiel

Ingredients

8 James Kittow's Pen'n'Tinny
   Sausages
1 white onion, finely diced
2-3 garlic cloves, finely diced
1 sprig rosemary, finely chopped
½ tsp smoked paprika
2 small red onions, roughly diced
2 bay leaves
150g sliced chorizo, cut into strips,
   save 50g to garnish
1 heaped tsp tomato purée
60ml red wine
500g fresh tomatoes
200g tinned chopped tomatoes
400g chickpeas, drained and rinsed
2 large red peppers, deseeded and
   sliced into rings
Olive oil
Sea salt and black pepper
20g fresh coriander, picked
Zest and juice of 1 lime
Handful of rocket, to serve

Method

1 Preheat the oven to 200°C/gas mark 6.
2 In a thick-based saucepan, heat a little olive oil and lightly brown the sausages, then remove from the pan and set aside. Reduce the heat and sweat the white onion and garlic until soft and translucent.
3 Now add the rosemary, paprika, red onion and bay leaves (in that order), and continue to sweat for a further three minutes before turning up the heat and adding 100g of the chorizo (the extra heat really helps bring out the flavour). At this point I tend to drain away any excess oil.
4 Reduce the heat again, add the tomato purée and cook for a further few minutes. Add the red wine, increase the heat again, and add all the tomatoes and the sausages. Bring to a simmer, add the chickpeas and reduce the heat. Put a lid on and allow to cook for about 35-45 minutes, stirring regularly.
5 Take the red pepper rings, season with olive oil, sea salt and cracked black pepper, and roast in the oven for 15-20 minutes or until they start to blacken. Remove and set aside.
6 Remove the casserole from the heat and stir in the picked coriander and the zest and juice of a lime. Season to taste.
7 Ladle into serving bowls, garnishing with the remaining chorizo slices, the roasted red pepper rings and some rocket. Serve with fresh bread, such as focaccia.

Top Tip: The lime and coriander will really lift the dish, but these flavours can also be swapped for parsley and lemon.

Richard du Pille, Head Chef, Duchy of Cornwall Nursery, Lostwithiel

"The inspiration for this dish came from having a day-to-day household ingredient and adding to it to make a quick, colourful, summery dish packed with flavour.

When cooking, the key is to have all the ingredients prepared, then just follow the simple steps. You can add to this dish, or swap the flavours; it's versatile, so don't be afraid to try something new once you're confident with the recipe.

I don't think anyone could be a chef if they didn't love food. I enjoy the whole process, from taking a raw ingredient to the food leaving the pass; to start with some simple ingredients and turn them into a lovely meal is very satisfying.

I'm proud of our café here at the Duchy, and am excited to be part of the next stage, where we'll be growing some of our own vegetables and berries, and incorporating these into the menu. And with our new deli about to open, I feel that the future is bright!"

James Kittow, Butcher and Grazier, Kilhallon Farm, Par

"We have our own pedigree herd of Red Ruby and Dexter cattle, and work closely with a small number of farmers who produce pork, lamb and beef for us.

With more than 130 years of rich heritage, I'm proud to have been born into a long line of master butchers. We're passionate about providing only the finest products to restaurants, retailers and families who value top-quality meat. A big part of why I enjoy my job is getting to work with our great team.

My greatest achievement was winning Best Farm Manager at the South West Farmer Awards in 2016.

My hobbies include being a member (the youngest) of Lostwithiel Rotary Club, where we meet once a week. I also enjoy walking the dogs around the farm in the evening, relaxing with a beer, checking on our cattle, and enjoying the crackin' Cornish countryside."

Quick Bowgie brunch using James Kittow's produce

Recipe by Richard Killingbeck, Grill Chef, Bowgie Inn, Crantock

Ingredients

4 James Kittow's Cornish Beef
   Burgers
1 James Kittow's Cornish Hogs'
   Pudding
8 James Kittow's Pork & Proper Job
   Ale Sausages
1 black pudding
4 large tomatoes
8 local free-range eggs

For the sautéed potato wedges

4 medium-sized potatoes, peeled, cut
   into wedges and parboiled
Olive oil
Salt and pepper

Method

1 Preheat the oven to 200°C/gas mark 6. Drizzle the burgers with a little olive oil and place in the oven for 20-30 minutes, flipping them halfway through.
2 Heat a large frying pan with a drizzle of olive oil and cook the sausages slowly on a low heat for 15-20 minutes, turning occasionally until golden. After the first 10 minutes, increase the heat. Add the sliced black pudding and sliced hogs' pudding (remove the skin first by snipping with scissors). Cook for two minutes each side until slightly crispy.
3 Pop all the cooked sausages on a tray in the bottom of the oven to keep warm, as well as four large plates in preparation for serving.
4 Cut the tomatoes in half, season with salt and pepper, and drizzle with olive oil. Place cut-side down in the pan and cook without moving for two minutes. Turn over and season again. Cook for a further two minutes until tender.
5 Break the eggs into the pan, turn the heat down, then baste hot fat over the eggs to lightly cook the tops. After about one minute, remove the eggs and tomatoes.

To make the sautéed wedges

1 Heat plenty of oil in a large non-stick frying pan until you can feel a strong heat rising.
2 Add the parboiled wedges in a single layer. Turn the heat to medium-high, so that the potatoes sizzle. Allow them to brown underneath.
3 Turn evenly two or three times until nicely browned – this can take about five minutes. Lift out and drain onto kitchen paper. Sprinkle with salt and serve.

Richard Killingbeck, Grill Chef, Bowgie Inn, Crantock

"Hearty pub food is the inspiration for this dish, which is super-easy to prepare. I've never worked with James Kittow before, and this is the first time using this produce, but I'll surely work with him again.

The ingredients in this dish speak for themselves and make a perfect, hearty brunch. I would serve this with a good, strong coffee, Cornish Ale, or even a Bloody Mary.

Knowing our customers enjoy what we do and knowing we make people happy is such a great part of the job. A career highlight: being in this book!"

"Knowing our customers enjoy what we do and knowing we make people happy is such a great part of the job. A career highlight: being in this book!"

Tomato ketchup

Making your own ketchup is easier than you might think,
and just as tasty as the shop-bought versions

Ingredients

1 large red onion, roughly chopped
2 garlic cloves, chopped
1 tbsp oil
1kg ripe tomatoes, roughly chopped
½ cinnamon stick
½ tsp ground coriander
½ tsp allspice
2 bay leaves
1 tsp dried thyme
50g caster sugar
Splash of Worcestershire sauce
150ml red wine vinegar
Salt and pepper

Method

1 Heat the oil in a saucepan and cook the onions and garlic for about five minutes until soft. Add a splash of water if they look like they are starting to catch on the bottom.
2 Add all the other ingredients except the vinegar. Season well with salt and pepper. Simmer for 15 minutes. Add the vinegar, turn up the heat and cook for a further five minutes.
3 Turn off the heat and blitz with a stick blender.

Summer stew with pan-seared cod and Deli Farm Charcuterie Cornish Coppa lardons

Recipe by Matthew Rowe, Chef/Proprietor,
The Falmouth Packet Inn, Rosudgeon

Ingredients

4 cod loin portions (hake is a good alternative)
16 Cornish new potatoes, parboiled, whole or halved
3oz butter
100g Cornish Coppa, cut into lardons
A drop of oil for frying
200g fresh kale
16 asparagus spears
100g garden peas (fresh or frozen)
200g broad beans, peeled
12 tenderstem broccoli florets
175ml good white wine
Salt and pepper
250ml double cream
1 lemon

Method

1 In a large frying pan, heat the oil and gently fry the potatoes until golden brown. Add the butter, lardons and cod loin portions, then season. Fry the cod, skin-side down, for approximately four minutes before turning them over and cooking for a further two minutes. Remove the cod, potatoes and lardons and allow to rest in a warm oven (about 120°C/gas mark ½).

2 Quickly add the broccoli, asparagus, broad beans and peas to the pan, and toss. Add the kale and the white wine, and bring to the boil, maintaining the simmer until the liquid has reduced by half. Add the cream, check the seasoning, and reduce a little more.

3 Divide the stew into four bowls, arrange the potatoes around the edge, and place the cod on top. Garnish with a fresh lemon wedge and lardons.

Deli Farm Charcuterie Chorizo and Parmesan potato cakes

Recipe by Matthew Rowe, Chef/Proprietor,
The Falmouth Packet Inn, Rosudgeon

Ingredients

100g semi-cured chorizo from Deli
   Farm Charcuterie, diced
1 bunch spring onions, finely sliced
400g cold, mashed potato
90g Parmesan
2 sprigs fresh dill, picked
Cornish rapeseed oil, for frying
Salt and pepper
Dill mayonnaise, to serve

For the breadcrumb mix

100g Panko breadcrumbs
4 eggs, beaten
20g ground rice or flour

Method

1 In a bowl, mix the mashed potato, spring onions, picked dill, Parmesan, and salt and pepper.
2 Heat a little oil in a pan, and gently fry the chorizo. Once done, add the chorizo to the ingredients in the bowl and mix well. Divide into four, and mould into burger-shaped patties about an inch deep.
3 Sprinkle the ground rice/flour onto one plate, the breadcrumbs onto another, and beat the eggs in a bowl. One at a time, carefully dredge the potato cakes first in the flour, then dip them in the beaten eggs, then roll in the breadcrumbs until completely coated. Fry the crumbed cakes in the oiled pan that the chorizo was cooked in, turning every two minutes until golden brown on both sides (you could finish them off in the oven to ensure they're hot right through).
4 Remove from the pan and drain. Serve with dill mayonnaise.

"I wanted to create dishes that are as comforting as getting a big cuddle from your mum!"

Matthew Rowe

Matthew Rowe, Chef/ Proprietor, The Falmouth Packet Inn, Rosudgeon

"I wanted to create dishes that are as comforting as getting a big cuddle from your mum! And to use the amazing fresh ingredients that surround us all the time.

I allow the ingredients to shine, and love anything fresh and local. We're blessed in our area to have so many good, local growers producing amazing ingredients, allowing us to make food to wow our customers. It really is down to the quality of the produce.

Unwinding is usually with a cold beer after work, and a day off is best spent with my wonderful wife (who's the real boss) or on the golf course."

Martin and Jean Edwards, Partners, Deli Farm Charcuterie, Delabole

"We are one of the UK's pioneering producers of air-dried meat. We supply to restaurants, delicatessens and farm shops throughout the UK, and attend a small number of food shows through the year. We also run an online shop.

The best part of the job is any new product development. Working with different meats and flavours is always interesting, but because of the length of time it takes our products to fully mature, one has to be very patient.

Our proudest moment was winning the Supreme Champion Product at the Taste of the West Awards in 2008 with our coppa, when our business was only 18 months old. Last year, we entered our coppa again and won the Champion Cured Meat class. Our most exciting time was gaining a contract to supply one tonne of our chorizo to the Athletes' Village at the 2012 Olympics."

Parma ham-encrusted pork tenderloin with a Polgoon Cider sauce and cider-poached apples, served with beans and peas

Recipe by Paul Stephens, Head Chef, The Mullion Cove Hotel

Ingredients

4 pork tenderloins (150g each), fat trimmed off
Olive oil
English mustard
4 slices smoked back bacon, fat removed (you'll use this for the crust) and meat diced
200g peas
200g broad beans, blanched and skins removed
500ml Polgoon Apple Cider
100ml white wine vinegar
3 cooking apples, peeled and cut into 20 balls with a melon baller
A squeeze of lemon juice
Salt and pepper
Apple blossom
Pea shoots

For the sauce

2 onions, peeled and sliced
Olive oil
1 star anise
500ml Polgoon Apple Cider
500ml chicken stock

For the crust

Bacon fat
100g Panko breadcrumbs
6 slices Parma ham, baked in the oven until crispy
Salt and pepper

Method

To make the sauce

1 Fry the onions in a heavy-bottomed saucepan on a medium heat with a little oil and the star anise until they start to caramelise. Turn the heat up to full, add a bottle of cider, and reduce by half.
2 Add the chicken stock and reduce until the sauce coats the back of a spoon. Strain through a fine sieve to finish.

To make the crust

1 Put a heavy-bottomed frying pan on a medium heat and add the bacon fat. Cook out until most of it has melted. Remove any solids left in the pan. Add the breadcrumbs and fry in the bacon fat until golden brown.
2 Crush the baked Parma ham into a dust using a pestle and mortar. Add this to the breadcrumbs, mix, season with salt and pepper, and remove from the pan onto a tray.

Continued on page 38...

To prepare the dish

1 Preheat the oven to 180°C/gas mark 4. Clean the frying pan and place back on a high heat. Season the pork with salt and pepper, and, in a little oil, fry for four minutes, turning often until there is an even colour all the way around. Remove from the pan, and while it's still hot, brush with mustard, then roll in the breadcrumb/ham mix until evenly coated. Place on a tray and bake in the oven for eight to 10 minutes, depending on thickness. Once cooked, remove from the oven and allow to rest for at least five minutes.

2 In the same frying pan, drizzle a little more oil and fry the diced bacon until crispy. Then add the peas and beans. Season to taste.

3 Mix another 500ml bottle of Polgoon Apple Cider with the white wine vinegar in a pan and bring to the boil. Add the squeeze of lemon juice and drop in the apple balls. Let them sit in the liquid for four to five minutes until they've softened but retain their shape. Remove from the heat and keep warm.

4 To serve, spoon the peas and beans onto the plate. Slice the pork at an angle and place on top of the vegetables. Place five apple balls around the pork and drizzle the sauce over the meat. Garnish with apple blossom and pea shoots.

"Pork and apple are always a fantastic combination – the crisp acidity of the fruit pairs perfectly with the tender, sweet pork."

Emma Clunie, Polgoon Vineyard and Orchard

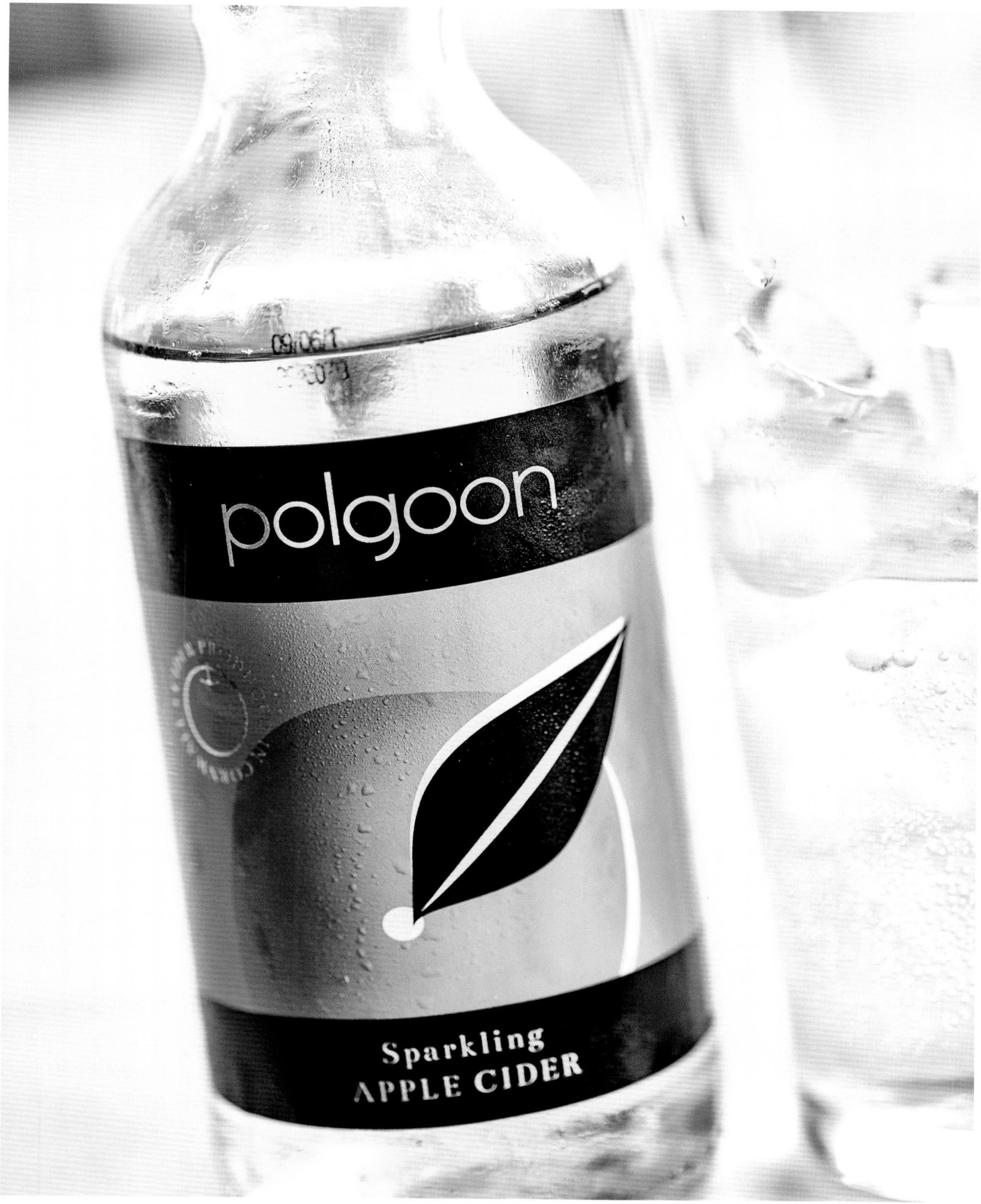
polgoon
Sparkling
APPLE CIDER

Paul Stephens, Head Chef, The Mullion Cove Hotel

"My favourite thing to eat with cider are pork and apples, so I was in my element with this recipe. We've worked with Polgoon for almost two years. They supply the hotel with cider, wine, juices and bubbly.

Be careful when adding the seasoning to this dish – keep in mind that the Parma ham and bacon are quite salty. My favourite ingredient is pork. Pretty much all of it is edible in one way or another, and we're incredibly lucky to have such great suppliers in the West Country.

The best part of my job is the freedom to be so creative with food, although you can get a bit carried away sometimes. The worst part is the unsociable hours – you need very understanding friends.

If I've had a stressful day, I find the best way to unwind is to go for a late-night drive, with the music turned up loud, singing along terribly. And, of course, the odd Polgoon cider when I get home is always a welcome relief."

Emma Clunie, Marketing Manager, Polgoon Vineyard and Orchard, Penzance

"Our vineyard and orchard in Cornwall grows and produces award-winning wines and ciders, as well as a range of artisan juices. We supply some of the finest restaurants, hotels, farm shops, delis and bars around Cornwall and the West Country, with a few selected outlets in London and the South East, including Fortnum & Mason.

The pork and cider dish created by The Mullion was delicious. Pork and apple are always a fantastic combination – the crisp acidity of the fruit pairs perfectly with the tender, sweet pork.

In my line of work, I love tasting the wine, and the process of perfecting each and every bottle. We're very proud of the fact that we grow and produce our wines here at Polgoon, and that most are Single Estate, something only a few vineyards in the world can claim. I also get to sample some of the best produce that Cornwall has to offer in our Vineyard Shop and our newly opened Vine House Kitchen. The worst part of my job is having to watch my waistline – those cakes and lattés are just too tempting!"

Cornish Duck Company duck breast with sticky red cabbage, squash purée and poached pear

Recipe by Thomas Hannon, Proprietor/Head Chef,
The Rising Sun, Truro

Ingredients
4 Cornish Duck Company duck
   breasts
Knob of butter

For the fondant potato
4 large potatoes, peeled
400ml chicken stock
Sprig of thyme
Salt and pepper
Knob of butter

For the butternut squash purée
1 butternut squash, peeled and
   deseeded
100ml cream
Generous knob of butter
Salt and pepper

For the sticky red cabbage
1 small red cabbage, thinly sliced
300ml red wine
250ml red wine vinegar
175g soft dark brown sugar

For the poached pear
1 pear, peeled, cored and quartered
400ml white wine
200ml water

100g caster sugar
1 cinnamon stick
2 cloves
1 star anise
Peel of half an orange

Method

To make the fondant potato
Using a 7cm-diameter circular cutter, cut out four discs. Cook in an oven-proof pan on a medium heat until they start to brown, then add butter, thyme and seasoning. Turn the discs colour-side up, add chicken stock until the potatoes are nearly submerged, then place in the oven at 180°C/gas mark 4 for 25 minutes.

To make the squash purée
Thinly slice the butternut squash, then sweat in a pan on a low heat with butter and seasoning. Once softened (but not coloured), add the cream and cook for a further five minutes, then blend until smooth. Put to one side until needed, when it can be warmed through before serving.

To make the red cabbage
Fry in a pan for three to four minutes on a medium heat. Add the red wine, red wine vinegar and brown sugar, and cook for a further 20 minutes or until reduced and sticky.

Continued on page 44...

To make the poached pear

In a pan, add the white wine, water, cinnamon stick, cloves, star anise, orange peel and sugar, and bring to the boil. Add the pear quarters and return to the boil for two to three minutes. Take off the heat, then leave the pears to steep in the liquor, turning them occasionally.

To cook the duck, and prepare the dish

1 Score the skin of the duck breasts in a criss-cross fashion. In a lightly oiled pan on a medium heat, place the duck breasts skin-side down, season and cook for six to eight minutes or until golden brown. Add the butter, turn the duck breasts over and cook for a further three to four minutes, constantly basting with the butter. (This will deliver medium-rare meat; increase the cooking times if you prefer your duck more well done.) Allow to rest for five minutes before slicing.

2 Place a dollop of the butternut squash purée in the middle of the plate, add a fondant potato disc, slightly off centre to the left. Spoon the red cabbage onto the centre of the purée, arrange the sliced duck breast on top of the red cabbage, and finally place a pear quarter so it leans across the fondant potato. Voila!

"Except for the meat, all the components in this dish can be made in advance. Perfect for dinner parties, so you're not stuck in the kitchen missing all the fun."

Thomas Hannon

"My wonder ingredient is most definitely butter – quite simply, it makes everything taste better!"

Thomas Hannon

Thomas Hannon, Proprietor/Head Chef, The Rising Sun, Truro

"Classic flavours and techniques often provide the inspiration for my cooking and menus, and it was no different with this dish – rich, autumnal flavours at their best.

Seasoning and taste-test throughout the cooking process results in the seasoning becoming integral to the finished dish. Taste-testing before serving should only be as a final check.

Working with passionate suppliers, like Roger and Tanya, is a fantastic part of being a chef – the ingredients are so important, so knowing that they're being produced or reared with integrity and care makes my job much more fulfilling... and a lot easier!

Winning Taste of the West's Best Dining Pub in 2016 was a very proud moment for me and my team at The Rising Sun. We were so thrilled to be nominated alongside some great pubs from the six counties of the South West, but to win was truly a big surprise."

Roger and Tanya Olver, Owners, The Cornish Duck Company, Truro

"We produce ducks from hatch to dispatch, supplying hotels and restaurants locally in Cornwall, Devon, and nationwide.

We supply Tom and Kate at The Rising Sun on a regular basis, but this is the first time we've worked together. This dish is great for a dinner party and, as Tom assured us, simple to cook.

The worst part of our job is the processing of the ducks, although we feel it's very necessary in order for us to retain our hands-on approach to ensure top quality. The best parts are when we walk around the farm and see the contented stock. We also enjoy attending a few food festivals because we meet a lot of our customers. We also love, of course, winning awards!

In 2007, we were asked to appear on *The Great British Menu* with two-Michelin-starred chef Michael Caines. We were excited, as well as being apprehensive, but Michael put us at ease with his down-to-earth, warm personality."

Crispy Cornish belly pork with St Ives Cider Apple Juice jus and apple-infused mashed potatoes

Recipe by Will Sherry, Head Chef, Boscastle Farm Shop

Ingredients

For the belly pork

1kg Cornish belly pork cut into 10-12cm squares (they must be scored — ask your butcher to assist you with this)
2 whole carrots
1 whole onion
Half a leek
1 Bramley apple
1 pint chicken stock
1 bottle St Ives Cider Apple Juice

For the mashed potato

4-5 medium-size Maris Piper potatoes
1 Bramley apple
125g salted butter
1 splash of milk
Salt and pepper to season

Method

For the pork

1 Preheat the oven to 180°C/gas mark 4. Roughly chop the carrots, the onion, the leek and the Bramley apple, and place into a deep roasting tray (there's no need to peel any of the vegetables or core and peel the apple).
2 Place the pork into the roasting tray, sitting it on top of the vegetables, then massage the pork rind with oil and a pinch of salt.
3 Add stock to the roasting tray along with the bottle of St Ives Cider Apple Juice and season.
4 Cover with tin foil and place in the oven for 30 minutes. After half an hour, reduce the oven temperature to 150°C/gas mark 2 for 3½ hours.
5 Remove from the oven and gently take out the pork, and allow to rest. Carefully sieve all the juices and vegetables into a suitably sized saucepan, discard the vegetables, return the juices to the heat and reduce by one-third.
6 Just before serving, place the pork back into a hot oven (200°C/gas mark 6) to crisp up for around 10 minutes.

For the mashed potato

1 Peel and chop the potatoes and place into salted boiling water.
2 Peel and core the Bramley apple, chop into 5cm pieces and gently cook in 15g of the salted butter until softened, not puréed.
3 Drain the potatoes, add the rest of the butter and a splash of milk, and mash. Season to taste.
4 Fold in the softened Bramley apple.

> ## "I've taken a lot of satisfaction from finding and using lost or unused orchards that had been left for years before we rediscovered them."
>
> David Berwick

Will Sherry, Head Chef, Boscastle Farm Shop

"The inspiration for this recipe came from tasting the ingredients I was using. The St Ives Cider company's apple juice made a great-tasting gravy to accompany the crispy belly pork and Bramley apple mashed potato.

The recipe is very simple. All you need to remember is that it's important to cook the belly pork for the time that the recipe instructs, and to crisp it at the end.

A top chef's tip is to remain calm. There's no need to get stressed over cooking, especially when doing it at home – it should be fun!

The best part of my job is using fresh seasonal ingredients, which include our own reared Red Ruby beef.

I unwind after work by spending as much time as possible outside, be it fishing or cycling, especially through the spring and summer months."

David Berwick, Cidermaker, St Ives Cider, Halsetown

"We grow apples to produce cider and apple juice. Our drinks are mainly available in Cornwall, but also in selected venues in London and the Home Counties.

I thoroughly enjoyed the dish created by the Boscastle Farm Shop – we polished off the lot! Absolutely fabulous.

The best part of my job is taking the product all the way from tree to shelf. Picking, pressing, fermenting and bottling it ourselves means I am hands-on for every step of the process. Nothing beats summertime in an orchard. It's not all idyllic mind you, but I'd happily choose a wet, muddy field over an office any day!

I've taken a lot of satisfaction from finding and using orchards that had been left for years before we rediscovered them. A great example is the museum orchard at Kirthenwood House near Hayle, planted years ago and long forgotten until new owners uncovered it. We use these traditional Cornish-variety apples to make a heritage cider which won Bronze in the 2016 International Cider Challenge."

Cream tea cheesecake

Recipe by Holly Olivey, Dessert Chef, Boscastle Farm Shop

Ingredients

100g digestive biscuits, crushed
25g unsalted butter
550g full-fat cream cheese
300ml double cream
100g icing sugar
50g clotted cream
1 plain scone
150g strawberries, hulled and
    quartered
6 tsp strawberry jam

Method

1   Grease and line an 18cm loose-bottomed tin. Melt the butter in a pan and add the crushed biscuits, spread evenly over the base of the tin and chill in the fridge.
2   Put the cream cheese, double cream, icing sugar and clotted cream into a bowl and mix until thick and combined.
3   Evenly spread a thin layer of the cheesecake mix onto the chilled biscuit base. Then dot a teaspoon of jam, pieces of broken-up scone and strawberry pieces over the mixture. Repeat this process, finishing with a layer of the cheesecake mix at the top. Decorate with strawberry pieces.
4   Put back in the fridge for three hours to chill before serving.

Devon

Waterside Bistro fish soup served with rouille, Gruyère and croutons

Recipe by Matt Buzzo, Chef/Proprietor, Waterside Bistro, Totnes

Ingredients

500g whole shell-on Atlantic prawns
500g salmon (on the bone is fine)
500g white fish (coley, whiting, pollock)
3 carrots, diced
3 onions, diced
3 celery sticks, diced
1 fennel bulb, diced
2 red peppers, diced
3 garlic cloves, chopped
50ml pastis (or Pernod)
250ml white wine
400g good-flavoured tomatoes (tinned is fine)
2 tbsp tomato purée
1 star anise per person
3l fish stock
1 pinch cayenne pepper
1 pinch saffron strands
Thyme, bay, parsley stalks
Gruyère, grated, to serve
Croutons, toasted, to serve
Rouille, to serve

For the rouille

100g cooked mashed potato
100g mayonnaise
1 tsp garlic purée
1 pinch saffron strands
1 pinch cayenne pepper

Method

To make the rouille

Mix all the ingredients together and leave for a few hours for the flavours to infuse before stirring again.

To prepare the dish

1 Preheat the oven to 180°C/gas mark 4. Roast the prawns with a splash of oil until the shells start to colour and you get the wonderful aroma of roasting shellfish (around eight to 10 minutes). Separately, in a large heavy-based pan, sweat the onion, carrot, fennel, peppers, celery and garlic in a little oil.
2 Once you have a little colour, add the wine and pastis, then all the other ingredients, including the fish and the prawns. Bring to the boil and simmer for one hour.
3 Allow to cool a little then blitz it all up with a hand blender until most of the fish, vegetables and prawns are blended in.
4 Push it through a sieve or conical strainer, discarding the solids. Season to taste with salt and pepper. Rinse out the sieve and pass again.
5 Serve with toasted croutons, grated Gruyère and rouille on the side.

Cheesecake made with Lemon Meringue Fudge from Roly's Fudge

Recipe by Simon Drew, Head Chef, Waterside Bistro, Totnes

Ingredients

100g Lemon Meringue Fudge from
   Roly's Fudge
6 digestive biscuits
50g butter, melted
450g cream cheese
100g sugar
2 gelatin leaves
Zest and juice of 1 large lemon
Fresh raspberries
Fresh mint
Candied lemon peel

Method

1 Grate the fudge until there are breadcrumb-sized pieces, and set aside.
2 Blitz the digestive biscuits in a food mixer until there is a fine crumb. Mix in the butter and half of the fudge, and then press firmly into the base of each mould. Refrigerate.
3 Soak the gelatin in cold water and leave for 10 minutes.
4 Mix the cream cheese, sugar and lemon zest, then add the remaining fudge.
5 Take the gelatin out of the water and add it to the lemon juice. Warm this gently in the microwave until the gelatin melts.
6 Stir the gelatin into the cream cheese mixture, ensuring it is evenly combined.
7 Fill each biscuit-lined mould evenly with the cream cheese mixture, tapping down to remove any air pockets. Refrigerate overnight.
8 To serve, garnish with a few fresh raspberries, mint and a little candied lemon peel.

Top Tip: At Waterside, we use individual metal mousse rings, but you could use a small 14cm spring-form cake tin.

Top Tip: When ready to serve, use a gas burner to gently warm the mousse ring, then push the cheesecake up a fraction first before allowing it to slide gently down onto the plate.

Matt Buzzo, Chef/Proprietor, and Simon Drew, Head Chef, Waterside Bistro, Totnes

Matt: "The team and I were excited when we were invited to contribute a recipe to the *Taste of the West Country* cookery book using Roly's Fudge. They have a magical little shop just up the road from us in Totnes; the sweet smell of cooking draws you in, long before you reach the door. Once inside, you can watch them making the fudge, tipping it out of the copper pans and working it on a marble slab.

We were asked to use their award-winning Lemon Meringue Fudge. I briefed Simon and Sous Chef Chris to create a dish that didn't lose the delicate balance of sharp and sweet you should find in a good old-fashioned lemon meringue pie, but which was still distinctly 'fudgy'. I think they did a pretty good job, and I hope you'll try their recipe.

The fish soup has been a favourite on the menu at the Waterside Bistro since the early days. I like to keep authenticity within my dishes, so I garnish with a spicy mayonnaise-type sauce called rouille, toasted croutons to spread it on, and finely grated Gruyère cheese, although a mature cheddar would work just as well."

Simon: "It's always fun to be challenged to come up with a recipe using new ingredients. One of the best parts of my job is liaising with our suppliers and checking the quality of the produce that we're offered. If you have the best ingredients to start with, you can treat them very simply and end up with a great result.

Among my favourite ingredients are the fantastic fresh fish and seafood we serve at Waterside. I live in Brixham, so it's great to have a connection to where that is coming from and to talk to our fishmonger about what's best to buy at any given time.

A top cooking tip is to always make the time for good, organised, quality preparation. It's vital in a busy professional kitchen, but without it, the home cook will also struggle to achieve a good result. Aside from that fundamental principle, when pan-frying fish fillets, leave the skin on, season with a pinch of salt, and cook all the way on the skin side. Only turn them once the pan is off the heat at the very end. You'll get lovely crispy skin, while retaining moisture in the fish."

Matt Jones, General Manager, Roly's Fudge Franchising, Exeter (and shop owner in Weymouth, Exmouth and St Ives)

"We produce crumbly, handmade fudge all over the country, with a large number of shops in Cornwall, Devon, Dorset and Somerset.

The best part of the job is visiting our shops and franchisees, as I get to travel to some lovely cities and coastal locations. The most difficult part is being forced to taste all the fabulous new flavours of fudge that we bring out... it's a tough job, but someone has to do it!

In 2017, I'm probably most proud of hitting our 30th year in business and seeing how Roly's Fudge has grown. This year, we've also won four golds for four different flavours at the Taste of the West Awards – a huge achievement to mark our anniversary."

"This year, we've won four golds at the Taste of the West Awards – a huge achievement to mark our 30th anniversary."

Exmouth mussels in a Crafty Cider, leek and bacon sauce

Recipe by Ian Middleton, Head Chef, Dukes, Sidmouth

Ingredients

1 garlic clove, peeled and sliced

6 rashers of smoked bacon, finely sliced

Olive oil

2kg mussels, scrubbed

200ml Crafty Cider

4 tbsp crème fraîche

1 small leek, chopped

½ packet of micro herbs (such as red amaranth and baby basil)

Method

1 Add a splash of olive oil to a large pan on a high heat, add the bacon and cook for a couple of minutes until golden brown and crispy.

2 Empty the mussels into a bowl. It's important to sort through them, tapping any open ones lightly on the shell to see if they close, and discarding the ones that remain open or any that are damaged, because these aren't safe to eat.

3 Tip the mussels into the hot pan with the garlic, cider, leeks and bacon, cover with a lid and steam for three to four minutes or until the mussels have opened, indicating that they're ready.

4 Add the crème fraîche, give the pan a shake, and bring to the boil.

5 To serve, pour the mussels into a bowl (throw away any closed ones), and sprinkle with the micro herbs.

Top Tip: Ignore cooking times. Instead, check dishes by using your senses (smell, taste and touch) to decide when they're done.

"For this recipe, I wanted to celebrate using mussels sourced from our Devon shores."

Ian Middleton, Dukes

"...being able to see a fruit growing on a tree following winter dormancy, then watching that fruit develop into something that we can use as producers to create a fantastic natural drink. It's a gift"

Dave Rowe

Dave Rowe, Head Cidermaker, Crafty Cider, Clyst St Lawrence

"I produce craft ciders made from traditional heritage apple varieties that are sold throughout Devon and the South West.

The best part of the job is the diversity that comes with cider-making; being able to see a fruit growing on a tree following winter dormancy, then watching that fruit develop into something that we can use as producers to create a fantastic natural drink. It's a gift. Being able to share and enjoy that with others emphasises the fact that I've seen the whole process through from beginning to end.

Standing in a warm orchard in early autumn, at the beginning of the apple harvest, is certainly a high point. However, that novelty often wears off by Christmas, when you're scrabbling around on all fours in the wind and the rain, trying to get the very last of the apple crop before it disappears again for another year."

Church House piccalilli served with Quicke's Vintage Cheddar ploughman's

Recipe by Isaac Cohen, Head Chef, The Church House Inn, Rattery

Ingredients

1 cauliflower, cut into small florets
½ cucumber, deseeded and diced
1 small white onion, diced
2 heaped tbsp table salt
1 small red chilli, finely sliced
250g caster sugar
400ml white wine vinegar
1 tsp ground turmeric
1 tsp English mustard
½ tsp curry powder
75ml malt vinegar
2 heaped tbsp cornflour

To serve

Quicke's Vintage Cheddar

Method

1 Place the cauliflower, cucumber, onion and table salt in a bowl, mix well and refrigerate for a minimum of three hours, or overnight.

2 Put the sugar, white wine vinegar, chilli, mustard, turmeric and curry powder in a large saucepan on a medium heat, stirring occasionally, and bring to the boil.

3 Rinse the salted vegetables and leave to drain.

4 Mix together the malt vinegar and cornflour to a wet paste and add to the saucepan.

5 Boil for a further minute, or until the mixture becomes thick, add the vegetables and stir until well coated.

6 Remove from the heat and leave to cool. Serve with Quicke's Vintage Cheddar and some chunky sourdough.

Top Tip: Store the piccalilli in sterilised kilner jars straight away and close the lid. This will create a natural vacuum seal as it cools and can be kept in the larder for many months.

"...I like playing with knives and fire, so for me, it was a choice between chef or psychopath. Fortunately, I chose to cook."

Isaac Cohen

Isaac Cohen, Head Chef, The Church House Inn, Rattery

"When I was younger, my dad used to buy piccalilli and have it with chopped liver — revolting!

I wanted to create a fresh, vibrant and delicious version, which I now love and eat most days. It goes perfectly with this strong, Vintage Cheddar. The turmeric has a great flavour and an even better colour, which gives the piccalilli its classic hue.

The best part of my job is getting to be creative every day. Also, I like playing with knives and fire, so for me, it was a choice between chef or psychopath. Fortunately, I chose to cook."

Stuart Dowle, Cheese Ambassador, Quicke's, Newton St Cyres

"We take enormous pride in creating great things from the land and delivering them to others in ways that evoke enjoyment. Our cheese is the perfect expression of this; it is our crown.

We've been making clothbound cheddar for five generations. We use our years of experience and skills to distinguish the flavour profiles of our cheese, to capture the best expression of the grass, soil and seasons. You can find our cheese all over the world, from the USA to Australia, as well as in selected supermarkets, delis and farmers' markets around the UK.

I simply love every single thing about what I do. Some of it's harder, some of it's easier, but I wouldn't be doing it if I didn't love every minute."

Pan-fried Eversfield Organic Lamb loin chops with crushed new potatoes, broad beans, garden peas and mint

Recipe by Steven Pidgeon, Head Chef, The Arundell Arms Hotel, Lifton

Ingredients

4 Eversfield Organic Lamb loin chops
   (approx. 125g each)
500g new potatoes
2 tsp olive oil
5g unsalted butter
1 sprig of fresh mint, chopped
30ml white wine
100ml chicken or lamb stock
2 tsp redcurrant jelly
100g broad beans (fresh or frozen),
   removed from their skins
100g garden peas (fresh or frozen)
Salt and pepper
Courgette flowers to garnish (optional)

Method

1 Place the new potatoes in a saucepan of cold water, bring to the boil and simmer for 10-12 minutes until tender, then drain and place back in the pan with a lid on to keep hot.

2 Heat 3g of unsalted butter and one teaspoon of olive oil in a frying pan. Place the lamb chops in the pan, season with salt and pepper on each side, and cook on a medium heat for six minutes (roughly three minutes on each side) until medium-rare.

3 Once cooked, remove the chops from the pan and place on a tray to rest. To the same frying pan, add the white wine and reduce by half, then add the stock and redcurrant jelly, and reduce until it achieves a sticky consistency.

4 Place the peas and broad beans in boiling water for three minutes. When done, drain the water and season, and pop the broad beans from their hard skins.

5 Place a saucepan on the heat with the remaining butter and olive oil, and add the cooked peas and broad beans, gently warming through. Next, add the freshly chopped mint and season, then leave on the side to keep warm.

6 Crush the potatoes with a fork, season and arrange in the centre of the plate. Place the lamb chops on top and surround with the broad beans and garden peas. Finish with the white wine and redcurrant jelly sauce.

"I can usually only manage half a day in the office. I love getting out on the farm more than anything…."

Mark Bury

Steven Pidgeon, Head Chef, The Arundell Arms Hotel, Lifton

"My inspiration for this recipe came from using the local produce from Lifton: new potatoes, garden peas and broad beans grown especially for the hotel.

Myself and Eversfield Organic have never worked together before, but you never know after this…

My top cooking tip for this dish is to serve the lamb pink and seasoned. In general, I think my best cooking tip is to season well – there's nothing worse than under-seasoned food.

The best part of being a chef is the buzz of a busy service. I unwind by taking the dog for a walk and enjoying a glass of wine or cold cider."

Mark Bury, Managing Director, Eversfield Organic, Bratton Clovelly

"Our 450-acre organic farm is on the outskirts of Dartmoor and is home to grass-fed native Aberdeen Angus cattle and Poll Dorset lamb. We offer an organic artisan grocery box delivery to homes across the UK, showcasing our own produce along with organic meat, dairy, fruit, veg and wild fish from other South West producers.

Although I've never worked with Steven before, I can often be found frequenting his restaurant, which is truly excellent. He's a chef who really knows his quality produce.

I'm proud of the significant difference we've made to the survival of rare-breed Aberdeen Angus cattle. This work was carried out using semen straws from the 1950s and 60s, with the help of the Rare Breeds Survival Trust.

Through our hard work on rehabilitating and nurturing our land, we've been seeing the benefits of composting in improved soil fertility and organic matter. Our soil is everything – it's at the absolute heart of all our work – so to see this transformation is truly astounding."

Bakewell cake filled with Clare's Preserves' Pink Exmoor Gin Marmalade

Recipe by Martin Ford and Richard Parsons, Owners/Founders, The Coffee Cabin, Appledore

Ingredients

For the shortbread base
125g salted butter (cubed)
55g caster sugar
180g plain flour

For the sponge
225g butter or margarine
225g caster sugar
225g ground almonds
50g plain flour
3 medium eggs
1 tsp orange extract

For the filling and decoration
1 jar of Clare's Preserves' Pink Exmoor
   Gin Marmalade
40g flaked almonds
75g icing sugar
5g butter
A few teaspoons of hot water

Top Tip: Be generous with the marmalade when assembling the layers.

Method

To make the shortbread base
1 Preheat the oven to 170°C/gas mark 3½. Grease three 20cm loose-bottomed tins and line with baking paper.
2 With an electric mixer, beat the butter and sugar until pale and fluffy, then add the flour. Combine on a low speed until it becomes a fine breadcrumb.
3 Press into one cake tin and smooth out using the back of a spoon. Bake for 15-20 minutes until golden.

To make the sponge
1 Into the same mixing bowl, add the butter, caster sugar, ground almonds, eggs, orange extract and flour, mixing until well combined.
2 Divide the sponge mix into the two remaining tins and make level. On top of each, dot and swirl with three teaspoons of the marmalade. Sprinkle one with flaked almonds. Bake both at 180°C/gas mark 4 for 25 minutes.

To assemble the cake
1 When all the components are cooled, first spread the shortbread with marmalade, then cover with the plain sponge, and spread the top with marmalade. On top of this, place the flaked almond-topped sponge.
2 To decorate, melt butter with icing sugar and add one teaspoon at a time of hot water, mixing until it is the consistency of double cream. Zigzag over the cake and allow to set. Enjoy!

Martin Ford and Richard Parsons, The Coffee Cabin, Appledore

"We opened The Coffee Cabin three years ago, and very quickly – and very unexpectedly – picked up recognition in *The Sunday Times*' food supplement.

Now, three years on and multiple awards later, including three consecutive Taste of the West golds, we're pleased to use Clare's Pink Exmoor Gin Marmalade, which inspired this recipe.

We are continually amazed by the support and love from our customers, and we're very excited for the future of The Coffee Cabin, as it's been a crazy ride so far!"

Clare Gault, Chef/Owner, Clare's Preserves, Bovey Tracey

"I'm an artisan producer of multi-award-winning sweet and savoury preserves.

I love people's reactions when they try our products for the first time – the pleasure on their faces is a delight to see. Winning awards is naturally a highlight, as it recognises the quality of our products, and the time and effort that goes into producing them."

Wild boar loin with Cox & Laflin Black Pudding Scotch egg, roasted baby beets and sweet potato duo

Recipe by Taran Rowse, Head Chef, The White Hart Hotel, Moretonhampstead

Ingredients

For the wild boar
400g wild boar loin or good-quality
  pork loin
4 slices Parma ham
Salt and pepper for seasoning
Rapeseed oil

For the Scotch egg
150g Cox & Laflin Black Pudding
50g Cox & Laflin sausage meat
4 duck (or chicken) eggs
1 egg, beaten
100g Panko breadcrumbs or good-
  quality white breadcrumbs
100g plain flour

For the sweet potato purée, fondant and vegetables
1½kg sweet potato
30g honey
100g butter
100ml chicken stock
16 asparagus spears
16 baby carrots
16 baby beetroot
Pinch of salt

For the stock sauce
1 carrot
1 onion
1 leek
2 celery stalks
½ garlic bulb
2 sprigs fresh rosemary
2 sprigs fresh thyme
20g tomato purée
Red wine
The bones and trimmings from the
  boar and a couple of marrow
  bones

Method

To make the stock sauce

1 Preheat the oven to 180°C/gas mark 4. Roast the bones for half an hour.
2 Peel and roughly chop the carrot, onion, leek, celery and garlic. In a pan, fry the vegetables with some oil and then add the tomato purée. Keep stirring until nicely coloured.
3 Deglaze the pan by adding a splash of red wine, then add the bones, rosemary and thyme, and cover with water. Simmer gently for three to five hours, topping up with a small amount of water if necessary.
4 Strain the liquid with a fine mesh sieve, discard the bones and vegetables, and skim any fat that has risen to the top. Add a splash more wine and reduce until the sauce thickens.

To make the Scotch egg

1 Bring a pan of water to the boil.
2 Thoroughly mix together the black pudding and sausage meat. Add a pinch of salt and pepper. Divide the mixture into four 50g balls and roll flat as round and even as possible.
3 Place four eggs into the boiling water for six minutes. Refresh in iced water, then peel.
4 Cover each egg with a round of meat mixture, close any gaps and shape it into one ball.
5 Using three bowls, first dip each coated egg into the flour, then into the beaten egg, and finally into the breadcrumbs.

To prepare the wild boar

1 Trim all the sinew away from the loin. Season with a pinch of salt and pepper.
2 Lay out four slices of Parma ham side by side, portrait-oriented, and place the loin lengthways one-third of the way down. Roll the closest end of Parma ham over the loin, then roll upwards. Slice into four portions.

To prepare and cook the potatoes

1 Cut the sweet potato into slices that match the height of a biscuit cutter. Using the smallest cutter (2cm in diameter), cut out 16 cylindrical fondants from the sweet potato. Don't discard the trimmings – instead, place them in a pan and fill with water until they're three-quarters covered, and bring to the boil.
2 Take the fondants and seal both ends in a frying pan until lightly coloured. Add the chicken stock and butter, and finish off in the oven at 180°C/gas mark 4 until soft in the centre and golden in colour.
3 Once the sweet potato trimmings are soft, drain the water into a jug and set aside. Add honey and salt to the trimmings, and blitz in a food processor until smooth, adding a little at a time of the cooking water to create a thick purée consistency.

To make the dish

1 Heat a frying pan with some rapeseed oil and seal the loin, turning evenly for one minute until a nice colour forms. Place on a baking tray in the oven at 180°C for seven minutes. Allow to rest for two minutes.
2 Deep fry the Scotch egg for one minute at 180°C or shallow fry for three minutes until starting to turn golden brown. Remove and finish cooking in the oven (180°C) for three minutes before turning and finishing off for a final two minutes.
3 Boil the beetroot in salted water for six to eight minutes. Peel, then add to the oven with a coating of honey and butter.
4 Warm the fondants through in the oven and boil the carrots for five to six minutes, adding the asparagus with three minutes left.
5 Arrange the fondant potatoes on the plate along with the baby vegetables. Slice the Scotch egg in half as well as the wild boar, and place among the vegetables and potatoes. Pipe the sweet potato purée in dots around the plate. Finally add the stock sauce.

Left to right: Andrew Cox, Taran Rowse, Sean Newton, Sous Chef, The White Hart Hotel

Taran Rowse, Head Chef, The White Hart Hotel, Moretonhampstead

"Real inspiration comes from those around you: from my Sous Chef, Sean, who cooks the best Scotch egg around, to Andrew Cox, a butcher who really knows his stuff. Incorporating produce from the local veg supplier and duck eggs from down the road, this dish is really about the character of Dartmoor.

Remember: good wine pairing, good ingredients and good company can make or break a meal."

Andrew Cox, Manager, Cox & Laflin Butchers, Ullacombe Farm, near Bovey Tracey

"I set up my business four years ago with my friend, Tom Laflin. I've worked in butchery since I was at school.

I started Cox & Laflin because I wanted to use the local farms that produce amazing meat. I love food and making sure that everyone can have the best produce. It really makes my day when my customers come back to tell me that the steak I sold them was the best they've ever eaten!

When I'm not at work, I'm on call as a retained Crew Manager with Devon & Somerset Fire & Rescue Service – it's a great feeling when you can really make a difference to someone's life.

To unwind, I like to keep fit by going to the gym four to five times a week. This definitely clears my mind and reduces stress after a busy day."

Ploughman's pasty

Recipe by Chunk of Devon, Ottery St Mary

Ingredients

For the shortcrust pastry (makes four discs for four pasties)
400g plain white flour
100g unsalted butter, diced
100g lard, diced
½ tsp salt
100ml cold water

For the filling
225g potato, diced (1cm)
80g white onion, diced (1½cm)
100g mature cheddar, grated
80g bacon, diced
22g tomato, diced
12g fresh spinach
48g Branston Pickle
1 free-range egg, beaten, for glazing
   (you could also use milk)

Top Tip: When making pastry, 'cold' is the word — cold lard and butter, cold water, cold bowl, cold hands.

Method

To make the pastry
1 Blitz the flour, salt and diced fats in a food processor for 15-20 seconds until it forms a breadcrumb texture. Keep the processor spinning, gradually add in the cold water and it will form into a ball. Now turn out onto a sheet of cling film, wrap it up and leave in the fridge for one to two hours.
2 When ready for the filling, slice into four. On a floured surface, roll out into thin circles, about 25cm in diameter (a dinner plate makes a good template).

To make the filling
1 Preheat the oven to 180°C/gas mark 4. Carefully mix the potato, onion, cheese and bacon in a large bowl. Add in the pickle and tomato. Finally, gently add the fresh spinach leaves.
2 Scoop even amounts onto each of the pastry discs, leaving a gap around the edge (for crimping).
3 Brush around the edge with the beaten egg or milk, then fold the pastry over to cover the filling. Seal down the pastry and crimp — start at one end and pinch the pastry together, then give a little twist to seal it.
4 Put a cut in the top of the pasty to let the steam out. Glaze with the egg or milk.
5 Place on a baking tray in the oven for about 45 minutes, or until crisp and golden.
6 Leave them to rest for five to 10 minutes and serve with a plate of salad or some chips. Or, enjoy cold on a picnic.

"...cool hands help to make great pastry."

Suzi and Simon Bryon-Edmond, Owners/Founders, Chunk of Devon, Ottery St Mary

"We always like to introduce a new summer recipe. As the Ploughman's is such a traditional and popular dish, we decided to see if it worked in a pasty. With the help of Richard Doidge, who is the 'chief kitchen hunk', we nailed it in almost the first tasting — bearing in mind that creating new recipes can take weeks, sometimes even months.

An important point to remember when trying this recipe is that cool hands help to make great pastry. This is delicious but don't be frightened to tweak it to your own personal taste. It's only a pasty — have fun! A final point to remember in the kitchen: don't juggle with knives, unless you're a knife juggler...

Our proudest moment would be winning Britain's Best Pasty, and the numerous awards we've won for our pies, pork pies and sausage rolls."

To unwind, the couple likes to cycle: "We both really enjoy our cycling, either down to the coast or over Dartmoor, mainly on the lanes," says Suzi. "Last year we completed a 700k cycle tour of Cuba, which was great fun."

Simon adds: "Our lads have just introduced me to golf, which looks like it could be a grin, but my passion from a young age has been watersports. In my formative years, I sailed as far afield as Hawaii and Bora Bora. Last year, I eventually managed to drag Suzi sailing around the Greek islands, which went down a storm (actually, there was no wind and it was really sunny). Most of the time we go out on our little boat, mackerel fishing out of Dartmouth."

Wicked Wolf Gin-marinated Exmoor venison with a gin, port and pomegranate sauce

Recipe by Daria Moughton, Owner/Chef, The Vanilla Pod, Lynton

Ingredients

For the venison
200-250g Exmoor venison loin
50ml Wicked Wolf Gin
1 sprig of rosemary
1 sprig of thyme
2-3 juniper berries, crushed
Sea salt and pepper

For the sauce
200ml venison or beef stock
100ml port
25ml Wicked Wolf Gin
1 tbsp pomegranate molasses
1 small shallot
1 sprig of thyme

For the salad
Bunch of watercress
1 red onion, sliced
Pomegranate seeds
1 tbsp lemon juice
3 tbsp extra virgin olive oil
Salt and pepper to taste

Top Tip: This recipe serves four as a starter, but you could add a side of new potatoes to make a light lunch.

Method

1 Season the loin on all sides with salt, pepper and crushed juniper. Chop the rosemary and thyme, and rub into the meat. Put the venison into a clean plastic tub and cover with gin, turning the meat several times. Leave in the fridge for 30 minutes or overnight.

2 To make the sauce, dice the shallot and add to a saucepan with venison or beef stock and a sprig of thyme. Bring to the boil then reduce to one-third (this could take around 10-15 minutes). Add port and gin, and reduce again. Season to taste, then add the pomegranate molasses. The sauce should be glossy in appearance and the consistency of a balsamic reduction. If you think it's not thick enough, put it back on the heat but reducing it too much will spoil the taste. Strain the sauce to remove the shallots and thyme. Set aside and keep warm.

3 Heat a frying pan to sizzling hot. Remove as much marinade from the venison as possible and pat dry. Add olive oil to the pan and fry the loin evenly until golden brown – about two minutes on each side should be enough for medium-rare. If that's too rare for you, just increase the cooking time slightly, but remember that venison is lean and cooking it for longer will dry it out.

4 When the venison is ready, remove from the pan, cover in foil and allow to rest for five minutes in a warm place.

5 To serve, mix the watercress with finely sliced red onion and pomegranate seeds, season with salt and pepper, lemon juice and olive oil. Slice the venison as thin as possible and arrange across four plates alongside the salad. Drizzle the port and gin sauce over the meat.

"The best part of my job is seeing the finished product in a bar or shop. It's so exciting seeing people order our gin at a pub, and hearing them ask for a 'Wicked Wolf and tonic' is a real buzz"

Pat Patel, Owner/Craft Distiller, Wicked Wolf Gin, Brendon

Daria (Dasha) Moughton, Owner/Chef, The Vanilla Pod, Lynton

"The inspiration for my recipe comes from Exmoor and its people. We are passionate about the place in which we live and work.

When you're cooking seared venison with gin and pomegranate, the most important thing is the quality of the meat. Find a good butcher, ask about the meat and its origin, and get the butcher to trim the venison if you're not sure how to do it yourself.

The scariest moment in my career was when we opened the doors of our café for the first time. It was a scary, exciting and proud moment for us. Since then, our business has changed a lot and has become a restaurant that we're very proud of.

After a gruelling season in our restaurant, we like to disappear to our retreat in Cyprus, where we enjoy the peace and tranquillity. But we also enjoy the beautiful scenery of North Devon's countryside, which we can only fully appreciate during the winter months."

Edward's Chocolate Orange Fudge brownie

Recipe by Zac Laverick and Sam Castle, Bakers, Otterton Mill, Otterton

Ingredients

270g dark chocolate chips
180g butter, unsalted
4 tsp coffee granules
1 tsp vanilla essence
180g brown sugar
3 eggs
135g Edward's Chocolate Orange
    Fudge
80g wholemeal flour

Method

1 Preheat the oven to 180°C/gas mark 4 and line a 20cm cake tin with baking paper.

2 Melt the butter in a saucepan. Dissolve the coffee granules with one teaspoon of boiling water. Add the coffee, vanilla essence and chocolate chips to the melted butter and stir until the chocolate has completely melted.

3 Whisk the sugar and eggs together until light and fluffy. Add the melted mixture to the whisked eggs and stir until completely combined.

4 Chop the fudge into 1cm cubes. Add these and the flour to the wet mix and fold until incorporated.

5 Pour the mixture into the lined tin and spread into the corners. Bake for around 40 minutes.

"To achieve the ultimate 'gooeyness', it's best to slightly underbake the brownie."

Zac Laverick and Sam Castle, Bakers, Otterton Mill, Otterton

"We're big chocolate fans, so the inspiration for this recipe was to infuse our famous chocolate brownie with the classic flavour of chocolate orange, with the added twist of the gooey fudge.

A top tip when preparing this dish is to have the egg mix and melted chocolate ready at the same time to prevent it from setting before you put it in the oven. To achieve the ultimate 'gooeyness', it's best to slightly underbake the brownie."

Edward P Bosworth and Scott Wilson, Edward's Fudge Kitchen, Dartmouth, Brixham and Plymouth

"We craft and sell traditional, award-winning fudge made in front of our customers on a daily basis. We have more than 30 different flavours and are always coming up with new and exciting ideas.

The most challenging part of our job is trying not to eat all the fudge, so our waistbands don't expand too much!

When we're not at work, we like to be outside in nature, cycling and running."

Banana loaf made with Chocolate Orange Fudge from Edward's Fudge Kitchen

Ingredients

2 ripe bananas, mashed
2 medium eggs, beaten
100g butter, melted
100g plain or soya yoghurt
100g muscovado sugar
Zest of 1 orange
200g self-raising flour
½ tsp baking powder
½ tsp nutmeg
100g pecans, roughly chopped
150g Edward's Fudge Kitchen
    Chocolate Orange Fudge, roughly
    chopped

Method

1 Pre-heat the oven to 170°C/gas mark 3. Grease and line a 900g loaf tin. In a bowl, mix the bananas, eggs, melted butter, yoghurt, sugar and orange zest until combined.

2 In a separate bowl, sift the flour, baking powder and nutmeg. Fold the dry ingredients into the wet mixture. Fold though three-quarters of the pecans and about half of the fudge.

3 Spoon the mixture into the loaf tin. Level the top and tap to remove any air pockets. Sprinkle over the remaining pecans and fudge, and bake for about one hour or until cooked (the fudge will go quite gooey in the middle, so bear this in mind when testing the cake).

Lyme Bay gilthead bream on crushed potatoes with chorizo and a cucumber, tomato and red onion salsa

Recipe by Franck Favereaux, Head Chef, Otterton Mill, Otterton

Ingredients

8 gilthead bream fillets, scaled and
    pin-boned
200g chorizo
800g new potatoes
100g wild rocket
Selection of micro herbs
Olive oil

For the salsa

2 tomatoes
1 cucumber
1 red onion
50ml balsamic vinegar
150ml olive oil
Salt and pepper

Method

To make the salsa

Deseed the tomatoes and cucumber, and chop into cubes. Dice the red onion, all a similar size. Mix with balsamic vinegar and olive oil, season with salt and pepper to taste and put to one side.

To cook the dish

1   Dice the chorizo and lightly pan-fry. Keep warm.
2   Boil the new potatoes until cooked but still firm.
3   Pan-fry the bream fillets in a little oil in a hot pan, skin side down for two minutes. When the skin begins to crisp, turn and cook for a further three to four minutes, depending on the thickness of the fillets.
4   To serve, crush the potatoes and, using a baking ring, place centrally on each plate. Take a handful of rocket and place in a ball on top of the potatoes. Balance two fillets, skin side up, on the rocket. Drizzle salsa over the fish and around the plate. Add the warm diced chorizo and garnish with micro herbs.

Top Tip: When cooking the fish, use a hot pan but take care not to overcook it.

"I wanted to use simple, fresh, local ingredients in this dish to produce a delicious plate."

Franck Favereaux

Somerset

Whole grilled Lyme Bay sole with Cornish new potatoes, caper nut brown butter and brown shrimps

Recipe by Olivier Certain, Head Chef, Clavelshay Barn Restaurant, North Petherton

Ingredients

1 lemon sole, skinned on both sides (ask your fishmonger to do this), head removed
400g Cornish new potatoes
125g unsalted butter
Olive oil
Cornish sea salt
Ground white pepper
1 shallot, chopped
Juice of half a lemon
1 tsp capers in brine
Handful of samphire
1 plum tomato, peeled, deseeded, diced
2 spring onions, diced
Handful of flat parsley
Mixed salad leaves
Small handful of peeled brown shrimps, precooked

Method

1 Boil the potatoes in salted water for 20 minutes until cooked in the middle. Once they've cooled, cut in half and roast in the oven with olive oil and 25g of butter at 180°C/gas mark 4 for 15 minutes.

2 Put olive oil, salt and pepper in a baking tray, add the fish, and season again. Cover the fish with 100g of butter, diced into small cubes. Grill for eight minutes without turning over but basting occasionally.

3 Put the mixed salad leaves on a plate, add the roasted new potatoes and top with the grilled fish. If you prefer, you could serve the potatoes on the side.

4 Take the butter the fish was cooked in and carefully pour all of it into a pan. Add the shallots, lemon juice, capers, samphire, chopped tomato, spring onions, parsley and shrimps, and warm through. Pour over the fish before serving.

Eggs Olivier, using Blackdown Hills West Country Eggs

Recipe by Olivier Certain, Head Chef, Clavelshay Barn Restaurant, North Petherton

Ingredients

4 free-range Blackdown Hills West Country eggs
Brioche or muffins
4 slices hot-smoked ham
150g girolle mushrooms
Fresh spinach

For the watercress purée
110g unsalted butter
400g watercress, leaves picked, half the stalks retained and finely chopped
Salt and freshly ground black pepper
200ml water

For the hollandaise
2 tsp freshly squeezed lemon juice
2 tsp cider vinegar
2 large free-range eggs, yolks only
Pinch of salt
125g butter, melted

Method

To make the watercress purée

1 Heat the butter in a pan over a moderate heat. Add the watercress stalks and season well with salt and pepper. Cook for two to three minutes until softened, then add the water and most of the leaves (reserving a small handful to garnish). Cook for one minute, or until the leaves have just wilted.
2 Allow the watercress mixture to cool, then transfer to a food processor and blend until smooth.
3 Pass the purée through a fine sieve and keep warm.

To make the hollandaise

1 Heat the lemon juice and cider vinegar until just boiling.
2 Place the egg yolks and a pinch of salt into a food processor.
3 Set the motor to run slowly, then gradually add the hot lemon and vinegar mixture to the egg yolks in a thin stream, until all the mixture has been incorporated.
4 With the motor still running, gradually add the melted butter to the mixture in a thin stream, until all mixed in.
5 Season to taste, with salt and freshly ground black pepper. Set aside and keep warm (cover the mixture to prevent a skin forming).

To make the perfect poached egg

1 Add a splash of white wine vinegar to a pan of water and bring to a simmer.

Continued on page 109...

2 Have another pan ready with hot water and salt.
3 Swirl the vinegar water, and put the egg in the middle for about three minutes. Next, put the egg in the salty water to remove the taste of vinegar. Poach each egg in turn.
4 Wilt the spinach, sauté the mushrooms, and toast the brioche or muffin.
5 Put some spinach on a plate, place the brioche/muffin on top, then more spinach, then the ham, followed by the egg.
6 Put watercress purée around the plates, along with the mushrooms. Pour the hollandaise sauce over the egg.

Olivier Certain, Head Chef, Clavelshay Barn Restaurant, North Petherton

"The inspiration for this recipe comes from the quality of the produce. It's a simple dish, which, when cooked well, can be outstanding.

The secret to getting the recipe just right is to not overcook the egg. And don't overheat the hollandaise, or it will split.

Working at Clavelshay Barn, cooking the food I love, and making people happy – that's the best part about my job. It's exciting getting fresh ingredients delivered and working out what I will do with them.

I unwind from work by walking with my wife, Mel, and our dog, Buster. And I enjoy a glass of pastis on a Sunday evening before dinner."

Furthermore, Clavelshay won the Award for No. 1 Place To Go in the Taste of the West 2016 Awards.

Dave Cooknell, Commercial Manager, Blackdown Hills West Country Eggs, Chard

"We are suppliers of high-quality, free-range eggs (no caged hens here), distributing throughout the West Country and to some of London's top hotels and restaurants.

A highlight is working with the talented, 'eggspert' (sorry, couldn't resist!) team of people at Blackdown Hills Eggs.

I enjoy cooking, and it's certainly handy that eggs are such a versatile food product for savoury dishes, and can be used to satisfy my incredibly sweet tooth. I also like working up an appetite on the squash or badminton court."

Pan-roasted Somerset chicken supreme with baby carrots, beetroot, green beans and sage and a Fussels Truffle Oil pesto

Recipe by Daniel John Williams, Bocabar, Glastonbury

Ingredients

2 chickens (French-trimmed)
Fussels Extra Virgin Rapeseed Oil
6-8 baby carrots
Bunch of baby beetroot
4 garlic cloves, skin on, roughly smashed
150g green beans
6-8 sage leaves, finely chopped
3-4 thyme sprigs
Balsamic vinegar
Unsalted butter

For the pesto

25g pine nuts
25g Parmesan
1 garlic clove, peeled
Fussels Truffle English Rapeseed Oil
Lemon juice

Top Tip: Ask your butcher to French-trim the chickens

Method

1 Preheat the oven to 190°C/gas mark 5. Top, tail and peel the carrots. Top and tail the beetroot but leave the skin on and cut into 1½cm cubes.

2 Place the beetroot cubes in a deep roasting tray with the thyme sprigs and the smashed garlic cloves, coat with oil and season. Cover tightly with tin foil and roast for 30 minutes.

3 For the pesto, combine the pine nuts, Parmesan and garlic in a food processor and blitz for a second or two. Add the truffle oil a dribble at a time with the motor running until combined and pesto-like. Finish with lemon juice and season to taste.

4 In a pot of vigorously boiling salted water, blanch the carrots for four minutes. Remove them with a slotted spoon, plunge into iced water, and return the blanching water to the boil. Add the beans, blanch for three minutes.

5 Place a frying pan on a high heat, coat the chicken in oil, season and fry skin-side down for one minute or until golden brown. Turn and place in the oven for 25 minutes. (If you have a cast-iron pan, put it straight into the oven. Otherwise transfer the chicken to a warm baking tray.)

6 After 30 minutes, the beetroot will be soft enough to cut or bite through, but still holding its shape. To it, add the carrots, a knob of butter and a splash of balsamic. Return to the oven for five to 10 minutes, until the vegetables are

Continued on page 113...

golden at the edges. Add the finely chopped sage and check the seasoning.

7 Remove the chicken from the oven and check for 'doneness'. Transfer to a plate and spoon over half the pesto. In the pan juices, fry the green beans. Add the remaining pesto to the green beans and mix well.

8 To serve, first make a little pile of the root veg. Tip the green beans over this (making sure all the truffley pan juices are distributed onto the veg). Cut the chicken into three pieces and arrange on top. Serve with sautéed new potatoes or a creamy gratin.

Daniel John Williams, Bocabar, Glastonbury

"I've always loved truffle oil, and, for me, combining it with pine nuts and Parmesan is always going to be a winner. A top tip when cooking: don't 'over-blitz' the pesto; it should be coarse and crunchy, not paste-like. Another tip: get a good knife, and keep it sharp.

Fussels has supplied Bocabar for many years, and its oils feature in a number of our recipes. The flavoured oils – chilli, smoked and garlic – are great for adding a subtle twist that lifts a dish out of the ordinary.

My most dangerous moment as a chef was probably angering the Mess Sergeant of an army barracks' kitchen by covering the pastry section in custard!"

Tim Fussell, Sales and Production Manager, Fussels Fine Foods, Rode

"We grow oilseed rape in a break crop within our four-year cropping rotation, and supply various farm shops and supermarkets in Cornwall, Devon, Dorset, Somerset, Gloucestershire, Wiltshire, Hampshire and online.

A highlight of my job is seeing our product on the shelves, especially when you're somewhere you didn't know stocks it.

Building our new premises is another recent plus point – when we switched on our new three-stage filtration system and it worked, that was a great feeling! Every day is exciting here at Fussels, we have a great team.

Outside work, I love to watch my kids do their thing – rugby, cricket, horse riding – but my own passion, above all else, has to be skiing."

Slow-cooked Coombe Farm Organic Lamb with a ricotta, fennel, lemon, spring onion and watercress salad

Recipe by Steven Mesher, Head Chef, The Queens Arms, Sherborne

Ingredients

4 Coombe Farm Organic Lamb neck
    fillets (225g each)
250ml red wine
3l brown chicken stock
50ml organic rapeseed oil
Zest and juice of 2 lemons
2 fennel heads
Bunch of spring onions
120g ricotta, diced
125g watercress
Sea salt
Cracked black pepper

Method

1 First season the lamb neck fillets and then seal the meat in a hot pan with a little oil. When done, deglaze the pan with red wine and reduce. Cover with chicken stock and cook on a low heat for three hours.

2 Remove the lamb and reduce the sauce until it achieves a thick consistency. Add the zest and juice of one of the lemons, and the rapeseed oil – this is now the dressing for the salad.

3 Finely shred the fennel and spring onions. Add the juice and zest of the remaining lemon, and season with salt and pepper.

4 Mix the diced ricotta in a bowl with the watercress, plus the fennel and spring onion mix, and add the dressing. Turn out onto a plate.

5 Slice the lamb and lie on top of the salad.

Top Tip: It's important not to overcook the lamb, and not to reduce the sauce too much. Always to season before and after cooking the ingredients.

"I was inspired to create this recipe as I wanted to produce a taste of seasonal, local produce."

Ben White, Steven Mesher and Olivia Sparks, Marketing and Sales Officer, Coombe Farm Organic

"In my job, it's exciting to see fresh produce delivered to our back door. And it's a really proud moment when I see my junior members of staff achieve greatness."

Steven Mesher, Head Chef, The Queens Arms

Ben White, Founder, Coombe Farm Organic, Crewkerne

"We produce organic beef and lamb, and also work with producers of organic chicken, organic pork and organic salmon. We source sustainable line-caught fish from a well-known fish market in Devon, before selling our produce online. We also sell some produce wholesale to various pubs, restaurants and hotels.

Although we've never worked with The Queens Arms, we have a lot of admiration for them. It's the first place we recommend to anyone travelling to see us in Somerset.

I think my career highlight has been winning Taste of the West gold medals in our first two years – it fills us all with pride.

I unwind from work by cooking – so you could say, I never really stop working!"

Pork, Honey & Mustard sausages from P&K Meats, served with celeriac mash and apple sauce

Recipe by Mike Dagger, Head Chef, The Lordleaze Hotel, Chard

Ingredients

4 P&K Meats Pork, Honey & Mustard sausages
1 celeriac, peeled and diced
Knob of butter
Salt and pepper

For the apple sauce

6 large cooking apples, peeled and diced
50g caster sugar
2 tbsp water

Method

1 Preheat the oven to 180°C/gas mark 4. Put the sausages in a baking tray and cook for 15-20 minutes, turning halfway through.
2 Peel and dice a celeriac, place in a saucepan and cover with water. Simmer for about 15 minutes, or until tender. Mash, then add a good knob of butter and season to taste.

To make the apple sauce

1 Place the diced apples in a microwave-proof dish with the caster sugar (you can adjust the amount, depending on how sweet you like your sauce) and two tablespoons of water.
2 Heat on full power until the apples are tender, then mash. For a thinner sauce, just add a little more water.

Top Tip: Taking under 30 minutes to prepare, this dish is an ideal midweek supper.

Paul Jeffery, P&K Meats

Mike Dagger, Head Chef, The Lordleaze Hotel, Chard

"The inspiration for this dish comes from our own Bangers in the Bar – we run a build-your-own sausage dish/menu at our Hotel, which is extremely popular.

When cooking this dish, remember that celeriac can hold a lot of water, so make sure it's fluffy and dry to get the best results.

One of my top kitchen tips is to never use a damp cloth for a hot pan!

Although my days are long, they are full of great tastes."

Paul Jeffery, Proprietor, P&K Meats, Street

"We are a butcher's supplying meat products to the public, restaurants, hotels, schools and various catering establishments in Somerset and surrounding counties. We make our own sausages and cure our own bacon, as well as producing beef, pork, lamb, poultry, game and other cooked and cured meats.

I enjoy all aspects of my job, including working with chefs, creating and designing new products, butchering and preparing products, talking to retail customers and, of course, sampling products."

Dorset

Beetroot tarte tatin with Symondsbury Produce Spiced Beetroot & Orange Chutney, watercress salad and goats' cheese

Recipe by Guy Horley, Head Chef, The Acorn Inn, Evershot

Ingredients

75g golden caster sugar
40g butter
A splash of sherry vinegar
1 tbsp honey
6 thyme sprigs
4 fresh beetroot, cooked
250g puff pastry
4 slices of goats' cheese (I've used
    Tor goats' cheese)
Symondsbury Produce Spiced
    Beetroot & Orange Chutney
Watercress salad
Salt and black pepper

Method

1 Preheat the oven to 180°C/gas mark 4. Place a small, oven-safe frying pan over a medium heat. Add the sugar to the pan and stir until it dissolves, then add a generous pinch of salt, all the butter and a splash of sherry vinegar. Keep stirring until it has turned brown (take care not to let the sugar burn).

2 Add the honey to the pan. Pick the thyme leaves from six stalks and add them in. Remove from the heat and stir.

3 Cut the cooked beetroot into nice fat slices and carefully (so you don't burn your fingers) arrange all the slices on top of the caramel in the pan, working from the edge to the centre in a spiral pattern. Season with salt and pepper.

4 On a lightly floured work surface, roll out the puff pastry so it's big enough to cover the beetroot, then place it on top, tucking the edges down into the pan. Put the whole lot into the oven for about 30 minutes or until the pastry is golden.

5 Wearing oven gloves, place an upturned plate over the frying pan (it should be bigger than the pan) and, holding the two together, flip the lot over. Leave it for 30 seconds to let the caramel mostly fall from the pan onto the plate, then slowly lift the pan.

6 Serve with dressed watercress, a slice of goats' cheese and a large spoonful of Symondsbury Spiced Beetroot & Orange Chutney.

> ## "Don't be tempted to dip a finger in to taste [hot caramel] – it will burn!"
>
> Guy Horley

Guy Horley, Head Chef, The Acorn Inn, Evershot

"I just love using fresh, local produce like the beetroot from our kitchen garden, and also the spicy fresh taste of this chutney.

The main thing to consider when cooking this is to watch out for the hot caramel. Don't be tempted to dip a finger in to taste – it will burn! Also, read the recipe through a couple of times to make sure you understand timings, cooking, processes, and so forth.

I'm constantly proud of myself and my team for the way we keep up with trends, and how we overcome obstacles each day but still put out a top-class product."

Elaine Duncan, Produce Development Manager, Symondsbury Estate, near Bridport

"We have an estate garden and orchards, from where we pick fruit and herbs for some of our preserves. Apples are picked from the orchards to press for apple juice, and I source seasonal fruit from local residents and community orchards.

There's a production kitchen on the estate and we make all Symondsbury Produce items from here, including chutneys, marmalades, jams, oatcakes, shortbread, rosemary spiced nuts, Scotch eggs, quiches, hummus, falafels and pesto.

I supply Symondsbury Kitchen with chutney, jam, marmalade and oatcakes for their menu, and Symondsbury Store with all products to sell to customers. The preserves are also included in our welcome hampers for our Holiday Cottages. I have an open door to my kitchen most afternoons to allow customers and visitors to sample and buy products."

Conker Spirit Dorset Dry Gin-cured sea trout with a tonic gel and cucumber sorbet

Recipe by Robert Ndungu, Head Chef, The Acorn Inn, Evershot

Ingredients

500g side of sea trout, trimmed
10 black peppercorns
15 coriander seeds
10 juniper berries
1 packet of fresh dill
Zest of 1 lime
Zest of 1 lemon
150g sea salt
50ml Conker Spirit Dorset Dry Gin
50g sugar
Sprigs of fresh dill, to serve

For the cucumber sorbet

3 cucumbers, peeled
300g sugar
300ml of water
50g glucose
Juice of half a lemon

For the tonic gel

225ml tonic water
50ml water
4g glucose
6g sugar
Pinch of salt

Method

To prepare the sea trout

1 Toast the spices and crush. Blitz the zest, spices, dill and 50g of the sea salt to a coarse consistency in a food processor and transfer to a bowl. Fold through the remaining salt, the sugar and the gin. This is the cure.
2 Generously coat the sea trout with the cure and leave for 10 hours. When ready to serve, rinse the sea trout well and dry with kitchen paper. Cut the fish into 1cm dice. Discard some of the edges if they are too salty.

To make the cucumber sorbet

1 In a saucepan, bring the sugar, water and glucose to the boil. Once boiling, add the lemon juice. Once the sugar has dissolved, remove from the heat and leave to chill in the fridge.
2 Blitz the cucumbers in a juicer then combine with the chilled sorbet base. Churn in an ice-cream maker then store in the freezer until needed.

To make the tonic gel

Mix the tonic water, water, glucose, sugar and salt in a pan and gently heat until the sugar and salt are dissolved. Pour into a tray and refrigerate until set, then cut into small cubes.

To serve

Arrange the sea trout pieces in a ring with the tonic gel, add the cucumber sorbet on the top and garnish with dill sprigs.

> # "Don't get tied down by recipes – just use them as a guide."
>
> Robert Ndungu

Robert Ndungu, Head Chef, The Acorn Inn, Evershot

"For this recipe, I wanted to experiment with the flavour combination of fresh local fish with a Dorset gin.

The sorbet can be made in advance. Any leftover cucumber sorbet can be enjoyed on a sunny day as a dessert, too."

Rupert Holloway, Head Conkerer, Conker Spirit, Southbourne

"We are Dorset's first gin distillery. We hand-craft our Dorset Dry Gin as well as our Cold Brew Coffee Liqueur, which we supply to bars, restaurants and wine shops across the UK.

Robert and I hadn't worked together before, but I thought the dish he created was incredible – the flavour of the trout was so well balanced with the gin cure, and then the firm, sweet-like texture of the fish was sublime. And then this was all paired beautifully with a sweet cucumber sorbet. Very impressive stuff! Now that I've tried his Conker concoctions, I'm certain we'll do lots of exciting things together going forward.

It's all incredibly exciting, with the goalposts shifting from day to day as new opportunities arise. I feel most proud when I hear people talking fondly about Conker when I'm out and about. That's a real buzz.

As for unwinding, it's as simple as getting home to my family. Spending time with my two little girls quickly brings you back to earth and sets straight what's important in life."

Almond, mint and raspberry roulade filled with Lily's Produce Raspberry Jam

Recipe by Todd Moffat, Chef/Owner, Taste Brasserie, Dorchester

Ingredients

1 jar of Lily's Produce Raspberry Jam
4 free-range eggs
115g caster sugar, plus a little extra for dusting
50g self-raising flour, sifted
25g ground almonds
200ml double cream
A few fresh mint leaves
A few fresh raspberries, for decoration
Flaked almonds, toasted, for decoration

Method

1 Preheat the oven to 190°C/gas mark 5 and line a 23cm x 33cm tray with baking parchment.
2 Whisk the eggs and sugar until they've thickened up and tripled in size. Fold in the sifted flour and ground almonds with a plastic spatula (scrape around the edge and cut through the middle, folding the flour and almonds in very carefully so as not to lose the air in the eggs).
3 Pour the mixture into the lined tray, spreading it out evenly and smoothly. Bake in the oven for about 12 minutes – it should be golden brown, with a firm texture that bounces back after touching.
4 Place a clean tea towel on a work surface with a sheet of baking parchment on top of it and sprinkle with a little caster sugar. Carefully turn out the sponge onto the parchment, peel off the baking paper, and leave to cool for 10 minutes.
5 Whip the double cream and fold in the freshly chopped mint. Spread the raspberry jam on the sponge, leaving a 1cm gap around the edges, and then top with a thin layer of the double cream.
6 Starting with the long edge – and using the tea towel to assist you – roll the sponge. Be firm at the start to tuck the bottom edge in, and then roll, unwrapping the tea towel and parchment as you go. Sprinkle the sponge with a little sugar and decorate with a few fresh raspberries and toasted flaked almonds.

Top Tip: Place a tea towel under the parchment to make it easier to roll up the sponge.

> "During my apprenticeship in Cambridge, I made chocolate éclairs for Princess Diana – undoubtedly my proudest chef's moment."
>
> Todd Moffat

Todd Moffat, Chef/Owner, Taste Brasserie, Dorchester

"I've been working in kitchens since 1981 and opened our first restaurant, Moffat's, in Stony Stratford with my wife Louise in December 1996. It was 6 December, we only had four bookings, no other staff, no dishwasher and we ended up full! Louise and I were washing up and polishing glasses until 4am. We got more staff and bought more equipment, and luckily for us we were busy for the next five years, until we sold up and moved to Dorset to buy the beautiful Acorn Inn in Evershot.

We've owned the Taste Brasserie since 2006 and the Taste Café at Chesil Beach for four years.

In Dorset, we're spoilt for choice with great local produce and dedicated suppliers. In fact, we caught the mackerel used in this recipe from a beach in Abbotsbury.

During my apprenticeship in Cambridge, I made chocolate éclairs for Princess Diana and she personally thanked me for them – undoubtedly my proudest chef's moment."

Louise Prince, Lily's Produce, Swanage

"My Lily's Produce range has gradually evolved from one or two preserves, always following Gran's original open-pot method, but I like to experiment with new fruits or put a twist on the traditional, and I now produce more than 20 jams and chutneys, many of which are available from local Purbeck retailers. Local produce is extensively promoted here in the community.

I like to think our family's passion for feeding people with good, rustic, home-cooked foods adds to the standard of the preserves, which transport you back in time, especially when one of our stalls pops up at a festival or local event and we make a little something to go with them. Our homemade cream teas, cakes, cordials (and bread pudding, in particular) are getting great feedback.

I suppose you would call Lily's a cottage industry: I grow some of my own fruits in a very small polytunnel in the back garden, and I love to forage for seasonal fruits.

Like I say on my preserve labels, everything really is 'lovingly made in Swanage'."

Mackerel tartare on toast with Wasabi Company wasabi

Recipe by Todd Moffat, Chef/Owner, Taste Brasserie, Dorchester

Ingredients

4 fresh mackerel fillets
1 fresh Wasabi Company rhizome
1 shallot, finely chopped
Small bunch of fresh parsley, finely chopped
2 tsp capers, rinsed and finely chopped
Juice and zest of 1 lemon
3 tbsp crème fraîche
Salt and pepper to season
Toast, to serve

Method

1 With a sharp knife, check the mackerel for any bones, then finely cut into pea-sized pieces. In a bowl, season the fish with salt and pepper, lemon juice and the zest. Add the chopped parsley, capers, and shallot in equal amounts, carefully mix with a spoon, and chill in the fridge.

2 Wash the wasabi rhizome and remove any knobbly parts. Holding the leafy end, finely grate onto a clean plate and leave for a few minutes to allow the flavour to develop.

3 Remove the mackerel mixture from the fridge, carefully stir in the crème fraîche and season to taste. Toast the bread, spread with the tartare and top with the fresh wasabi, a little at a time.

Top Tip: Only use the freshest mackerel and wasabi – and don't over-mix the ingredients.

Tom Amery, Managing Director, The Watercress Company, Dorchester

"We are growers of watercress, baby leaf salads and fresh wasabi. We supply retailers nationwide as well as specialising in local food service in the South West.

We are extremely lucky to have been featured on a number of television programmes over the years. As well as being a little bit embarrassing sometimes, it's a nice way to document our farming progress, especially with new projects such as our fresh wasabi."

Over the past few years, we've started raising money for local charities by running. 'Team Watercress' has now completed several runs, ranging in distance from 10k to marathons, including Paris, Venice, Athens and, of course, Dorchester. Our crops are the perfect training food, and research has shown that watercress repairs stress from exercise, which seems to be working for us! We find it's a great opportunity to relax, and many of our best ideas come to us while chatting on a run."

Nick Russell, Sales Manager, The Wasabi Company Farms, Dorchester

"We are growers of fresh wasabi and are the only commercial wasabi farm in Europe. We supply to chefs and distributors throughout Europe, and on occasion will have requests from further afield.

Real, fresh wasabi is still widely unknown, and a great part of my job is bringing this new product to so many people. The hardest part of the job is keeping the plants happy, year round. Being the only farm in Europe, there is not a wealth of knowledge out there to draw from, so we rely on trial and error when developing new ideas, and this can be pretty nerve-wracking.

We are lucky enough to work with some of the top chefs in the country - seeing your own product on the menu of a fine dining restaurant adorned with Michelin Stars... that's a pretty special."

Smoked trout with Watercress Company Baby Leaf Salad and watercress dressing

Ingredients

230ml vegetable oil (such as sunflower or canola) for cooking
1 large or 2 small shallots, finely sliced
1 tsp plain flour
125g smoked trout
¼ cucumber, seeds removed and sliced
12 cherry tomatoes, halved
12 caperberries
200g Watercress Company Baby Leaf Salad

For the dressing

80g Watercress Company watercress
100ml crème fraîche
50ml soya yoghurt
Zest and juice of 1 lemon
Salt and pepper to taste

Method

1 Pour the oil into a saucepan over a medium heat. Take care it doesn't splash up.

2 Coat the shallot slices in the flour, shaking off any excess. Drop a slice of onion into the oil to test – if it begins sizzling straight away and turns golden brown in about one minute, then the oil is hot enough. Tip the remaining onions into the hot oil – be careful as it will splutter a bit – and move them around in the pan so they colour evenly. Once they are golden and crispy, remove with a slotted spoon or tongs and drain on kitchen paper. Season with a little salt and set aside.

3 To make the dressing, wash the watercress and place into a blender with all the other ingredients. Season with salt and pepper, and blitz until it has a pouring consistency. Adjust the seasoning to your liking.

4 Wash the salad leaves and scatter between four plates. Top with the trout, cucumber, tomatoes and caperberries. Add a good amount of crispy shallots on top and drizzle over the dressing before serving.

Wiltshire

6X Gold ale-steamed mussels with whipped citrus tarragon butter and chilli-crusted gluten-free 6X Gold beer bread

Recipe by Scott Ferguson, Food Development Manager, Wadworth & Co. Brewery, Devizes

Ingredients

For the mussels

2kg whole shell fresh mussels – buy and cook them on the same day
400ml Wadworth 6X Gold gluten-free golden ale
100ml double cream
100g banana shallots, finely diced
200g samphire
40g Dijon mustard
2 garlic cloves, minced
Pinch of salt and pepper

For the tarragon butter

100g unsalted butter, softened
25ml whole milk
Zest and juice of half a lemon
Zest and juice of half a lime
20g fresh tarragon

For the beer bread

350ml Wadworth 6X Gold
1 red chilli, deseeded and finely chopped
1 green chilli, deseeded and finely chopped
3 tbsp maple syrup
300g gluten-free flour
105g buckwheat flour
2½ tsp xanthan gum
1 tsp salt
3 medium eggs, room temperature
3 tbsp vegetable oil
1 tsp cider vinegar
2¼ tsp fast-action dried yeast
50g butter, to grease the tin

Method

To make the tarragon butter

1 Using a hand-held whisk mixer, combine the softened butter and milk together on a low level for two minutes, then add the lemon and lime zest.

2 In a food processor, blend the tarragon and the lemon and lime juice to a paste and add to the butter mix. Now blend on full power until whipped, light and fluffy.

To make the beer bread

1 Preheat the oven to 190°C/gas mark 5 and grease a 22cm x 12cm loaf tin with butter.

2 Mix the flour, buckwheat, xanthan gum and salt together in a bowl. In a separate bowl, beat together the eggs, vegetable oil, maple syrup and cider vinegar.

3 Using an electric mixer, add the flour mix to the egg mix and whisk until there is a smooth batter. Whisk in the beer and yeast at a high speed for at least four minutes.

4 Pour the mixture into the loaf tin and sprinkle with the chopped chilli. Cover with a sheet of buttered greaseproof paper and leave to rise for 45-60 minutes or until it has doubled in volume.

5 Bake in the middle of a preheated oven for 35-45 minutes until firm to the touch and lightly coloured. When done, leave to cool.

Cooking and serving

1 Scrub the mussels in plenty of cold water to remove barnacles and sand, discard any that float to the top or that don't close when given a sharp tap with a knife, as they are dead. Make sure to remove the beard (a fibrous clump of hairs that sprouts from the shell); you can do this by giving it a sharp tug towards the hinge end. Once cleaned, place in a bowl of fresh cold water until ready to use (it's a good idea to change this water a couple of times as it helps to remove any sand or salt before cooking).

2 Place a large heavy-bottomed pan on the heat with a lid for about three to six minutes – you want the pan to be very hot so it steams the mussels quickly. Add the mussels, shallots and beer, replace the lid and leave to steam for two minutes, giving the pot the occasional shake.

3 Add the garlic, seasoning, mustard and cream, and place the lid back on for a further two minutes until it comes back to the boil and all the mussels have opened. Then add samphire and two to three knobs of the whipped tarragon butter. Stir and shake to mix together.

4 Pour mussels and plenty of the beer sauce into mussel pots or a large bowl with a lid – this could sit in the middle of the table for all your guests to share, with the lid used for the discarded shells.

5 Slice the beer bread and spread with whipped citrus tarragon butter – delicious to dip in the sauce while scoffing lots of mussels!

Scott Ferguson, Food Development Manager, Wadworth & Co. Brewery, Devizes

"This recipe of beer and mussels has the additional flavours of chilli and citrus, which help to bring out the hoppy ale aroma. It's delicious to dip the bread in the sauce. So simple, so messy and so tasty, but, more importantly, it's so much fun sharing with friends and family.

I have so many ingredients I love to work with, but as long as they're fresh, regional and in season, I'll create a dish.

My main piece of advice to those interested in cooking is that everyone can cook, so just listen, read and follow. Use a sharp knife, a hot pan, season well, keep on cooking and give it a go!

My proudest moment was when my 16-year-old son decided to become a chef – he now has a place on the Royal Academy of Culinary Arts' Specialised Chefs' Scholarship."

"...everyone can cook... use a sharp knife, a hot pan, season well... and give it a go!"

Helen Browning's Organic Bacon, crab and herb hotcakes, with poached eggs and crème fraîche

Recipe by Paul Winch, Head Chef, Royal Oak, Bishopstone

Ingredients

100g Helen Browning's Organic Smoked Back Bacon
100g white crab meat
100g self-raising flour, sieved
75g strong cheddar, grated
2 tbsp herbs (such as parsley, basil and dill), finely chopped
6 eggs (4 for poaching, 2 beaten for the hotcake mix)
6 tbsp milk
Salt and pepper
White wine vinegar
Olive oil and butter for frying
Crème fraîche to serve

Method

1 Put a non-stick pan on a reasonably high heat and carefully add the bacon – you won't need oil if the pan is hot because the bacon will cook nicely in its own residual heat. Fry until crisp, then allow to cool down before chopping into small pieces, then setting aside.

2 Put on a pan of water for poaching the eggs. Add salt and a few dashes of white wine vinegar.

3 Mix the flour, cheese, chopped herbs, crab meat and chopped bacon into a bowl, and season. Make a well in the centre and add the two beaten eggs and the milk, and combine to make a thick batter.

4 Wipe the frying pan clean with kitchen towel and put back on the heat. Add a little oil, then carefully drop two spoonfuls of batter (enough for one hotcake) into the pan. Cook on a medium heat until the edges start to cook, then flip over and keep cooking until nicely browned. Repeat the process until all eight cakes are made.

5 Now poach the eggs in the hot water until soft (around two minutes on simmer).

6 Serve two cakes in the centre of each plate, carefully place an egg on top, and add a dollop of crème fraîche on the side.

Top Tip: Try using streaky rather than back bacon: it is easier to get crispy.

"My greatest moment was achieving three AA Rosettes in a power cut, with everything melting as we worked. We had a full restaurant and not one person complained, including the inspector."

Paul Winch

Helen Browning, Founder, Helen Browning's Organic, Bishopstone

"There's a huge amount going on here. We have a dairy herd, lots of calves and beef cattle, 300 Romney ewes, 200 British Saddleback sows, 400 acres of cereal and pulse crops, and a small flock of laying hens. Our products are made from UK-farmed organic meat, are full of flavour and never have any fillers; all the hard work that goes into farming our organic pigs is reflected in food that feels and tastes good when you eat it. We supply organic pork products (ranging from pork cuts and mince to bacon, speedy sausages and hot dogs) across the UK to supermarkets, some well-known box schemes and, from time to time, export to customers across the EU. Of everything I love about organic farming – the wildlife, the landscape, the delicious food – what motivates me more than anything is allowing our animals to have as good a life as possible.

Paul and I have worked together for just over three years in both our pub here in the village and the Chop House in Old Town, Swindon. I regularly eat his fabulous food in the pub, and loved this recipe. Our back and streaky bacon is delicious however it's cooked…"

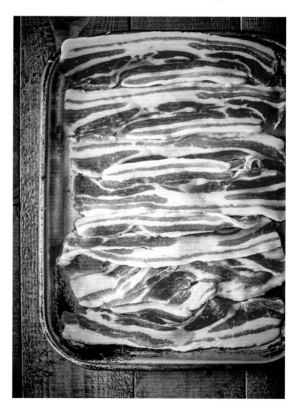

Thank you to the following Taste of the West
award-winners who made this recipe book possible

The Acorn Inn
01935 83228
acorn-inn.co.uk

The Arundell Arms
01566 784666
arundellarms.com

Blackdown Hills West Country Eggs
01460 234883
blackdownhillseggs.co.uk

Bocabar Glastonbury
01458 440558
glastonbury.bocabar.co.uk

Boscastle Farm Shop & Cafe
01840 250827
boscastlefarmshop.co.uk

Chunk of Devon
01404 814401
chunkofdevon.co.uk

The Church House Inn (South Brent)
01364 642220
thechurchhouseinn.co.uk

Clare's Preserves
01626 834696
clarespreserves.co.uk

Clavelshay Barn Restaurant
01278 662629
clavelshaybarn.co.uk

The Coffee Cabin
01237 475843

Conker Spirit
01202 430384
conkerspirit.co.uk

Coombe Farm Organic
01460 279509
coombefarmorganic.co.uk

The Cornish Duck Co. Ltd
01726 882383
cornishduck.com

Deli Farm Charcuterie
01840 214106
delifarmcharcuterie.co.uk

Duchy of Cornwall Nursery
01208 872668
duchyofcornwallnursery.co.uk

Dukes
01395 513320
dukessidmouth.co.uk

Eversfield Organic
01837 871400
eversfieldorganic.co.uk

The Falmouth Packet Inn
01736 762240
falmouthpacketinn.co.uk

Fussels Fine Foods Ltd
01373 831286
fusselsfinefoods.co.uk

Helen Browning's Organic
01793 790460
helenbrowningsorganic.co.uk

James Kittow, Butcher & Grazier
01726 814926
kittowsbutchers.co.uk

Lordleaze Hotel
01460 61066
lordleazehotel.com

Mullion Cove Hotel
01326 240328
mullion-cove.co.uk

Otterton Mill
01395 568521
ottertonmill.com

P & K Meats
01458 441439

The Queens Arms
01963 220317
thequeensarms.com

Quicke's Traditional Ltd
01392 851222
quickes.co.uk

The Rising Sun
01872 240003
risingsuntruro.co.uk

Symondsbury Estate
01308 424116
symondsburyestate.co.uk

Taste Brasserie
01305 257776
tastebrasserie.co.uk

The Vanilla Pod Restaurant
01598 753706
thevanillapodlynton.co.uk

The Watercress Company
01929 463241
thewatercresscompany.com

Waterside Bistro
01803 864069
watersidebistro.com

**The White Hart Hotel
(Moretonhampstead)**
01647 440500
whitehartdartmoor.co.uk

Wicked Wolf Gin
01598 741357
wickedwolfgin.com

Bowgie Inn
01637 830363
bowgie.com

Cox & Laflin Butchers
01364 661100

Crafty Cider
07966 757223
craftycider.co.uk

Edward's Fudge Kitchen
01803 852671
edsfudge.co.uk

Polgoon Vineyard & Orchard
01736 333946
polgoon.com

St Ives Cider
01736 795267
stivescider.co.uk

Wadworth & Co. Ltd
01380 723361
wadworth.co.uk

Lilys Produce
07403 340882
lilysproduce.com

Roly's Fudge
01392 201059
rolysfudge.co.uk

Almonds
Bakewell cake 76
Almond, mint and raspberry roulade 132

Apple
Parma ham-encrusted pork tenderloin 36
Crispy belly pork with apple juice jus 48
Pork sausages with celeriac mash 118

Asparagus
Summer stew with pan-seared cod 30
Wild boar with Scotch egg 80

Bacon
Parma ham-encrusted pork tenderloin 36
Mussels with cider, leek and bacon 64
Ploughman's pasty 86
Bacon, crab and herb hotcakes 150

Banana
Banana loaf 98

Bay leaf
Fish soup 56
Sausage, chickpea, chorizo casserole 20
Tomato ketchup 28

Beef burgers
Quick brunch 24

Beetroot
Wild boar with Scotch egg 80
Pan-roasted chicken supreme 110
Beetroot tarte tatin 124

Black pudding
Quick brunch 24
Wild boar with Scotch egg 80

Branston Pickle
Ploughman's pasty 86

Brioche
Eggs Olivier 106

Broad beans
Summer stew with pan-seared cod 30
Parma ham-encrusted pork tenderloin 36
Pan-fried lamb loin chops 72

Broccoli
Summer stew with pan-seared cod 30

Brown shrimps
Whole grilled sole with new potatoes 104

Butternut squash
Duck with cabbage, squash and pear 42

Caperberries
Smoked trout with baby leaf salad 140

Capers
Whole grilled sole with new potatoes 104
Mackerel tartare on toast with wasabi 136

Carrots
Crispy belly pork with apple juice jus 48
Fish soup 56
Wild boar with Scotch egg 80
Pan-roasted chicken supreme 110

Cauliflower
Piccalilli and cheddar ploughman's 68

Cayenne pepper
Fish soup 56

Celeriac
Pork sausages with celeriac mash 118

Celery
Wild boar with Scotch egg 80
Fish soup 56

CHEESE
  Cheddar
  Piccalilli and cheddar ploughman's 68
  Ploughman's pasty 86
  Bacon, crab and herb hotcakes 150

  Goats'
  Beetroot tarte tatin 124

  Gruyère
  Fish soup 56

  Parmesan
  Chorizo and Parmesan potato cakes 32
  Pan-roasted chicken supreme 110

  Ricotta
  Slow-cooked lamb 114

Chicken
Pan-roasted chicken supreme 110

Chickpeas
Sausage, chickpea, chorizo casserole 20

Chilli
Piccalilli and cheddar ploughman's 68
Ale-steamed mussels 144

Chocolate
Chocolate orange fudge brownie 94

Chorizo
Sausage, chickpea, chorizo casserole 20
Chorizo and Parmesan potato cakes 32
Gilthead bream on crushed potatoes 100

Cider
Parma ham-encrusted pork tenderloin 36
Mussels with cider, leek and bacon 64

Cinnamon
Tomato ketchup 28
Duck with cabbage, squash and pear 42

Cloves
Duck with cabbage, squash and pear 42

Cod
Summer stew with pan-seared cod 30

Coffee granules
Chocolate orange fudge brownie 94

Coppa
Summer stew with pan-seared cod 30

Coriander
Sausage, chickpea, chorizo casserole 20
Tomato ketchup 28

Courgette flowers
Pan-fried lamb loin chops 72

Crab
Bacon, crab and herb hotcakes 150

Cream cheese
Cream tea cheesecake 52
Lemon meringue fudge cheesecake 58

Crème fraîche
Mussels with cider, leek and bacon 64
Mackerel tartare on toast with wasabi 136
Smoked trout with baby leaf salad 140
Bacon, crab and herb hotcakes 150

Croutons
Fish soup 56

Cucumber
Piccalilli and cheddar ploughman's 68
Gilthead bream on crushed potatoes 100
Gin-cured sea trout 128
Smoked trout with baby leaf salad 140

Curry powder
Piccalilli and cheddar ploughman's 68

Digestive biscuits
Cream tea cheesecake 52
Lemon meringue fudge cheesecake 58

Dill
Chorizo and Parmesan potato cakes 32
Gin-cured sea trout 128

Duck
Duck with cabbage, squash and pear 42

Fennel
Fish soup 56
Slow-cooked lamb 114

Garlic
Sausage, chickpea, chorizo casserole 20
Tomato ketchup 28
Fish soup 56
Mussels with cider, leek and bacon 64
Wild boar with Scotch egg 80
Pan-roasted chicken supreme 110
Ale-steamed mussels 144

Gilthead bream fillets
Gilthead bream on crushed potatoes 100

Gin
Gin-marinated venison 90
Gin-cured sea trout 128

Green beans
Pan-roasted chicken supreme 110

Ground rice
Chorizo and Parmesan potato cakes 32

Ham (hot-smoked)
Eggs Olivier 106

Hogs' pudding
Quick brunch 24

Honey
Wild boar with Scotch egg 80
Beetroot tarte tatin 124

Juniper berries
Gin-marinated venison 90
Gin-cured sea trout 128

Kale
Summer stew with pan-seared cod 30

Lamb
Pan-fried lamb loin chops 72
Slow-cooked lamb 114

Leek
Crispy belly pork with apple juice jus 48
Mussels with cider, leek and bacon 64
Wild boar with Scotch egg 80

Lemon sole
Whole grilled sole with new potatoes 104

Mackerel
Mackerel tartare on toast with wasabi 136

Maple Syrup
Ale-steamed mussels 144

Micro herbs
Gilthead bream on crushed potatoes 100

Mint
Lemon meringue fudge cheesecake 58
Pan-fried lamb loin chops 72
Almond, mint and raspberry roulade 132

Mushrooms (Girolle)
Eggs Olivier 106

Mussels
Mussels with cider, leek and bacon 64
Ale-steamed mussels 144

Nutmeg
Banana loaf 98

Onion
Sausage, chickpea, chorizo casserole 20
Tomato ketchup 28
Parma ham-encrusted pork tenderloin 36
Crispy belly pork with apple juice jus 48
Fish soup 56
Piccalilli and cheddar ploughman's 68
Wild boar with Scotch egg 80
Ploughman's pasty 86
Gin-marinated venison 90
Gilthead bream on crushed potatoes 100

Orange
Banana loaf 98

Orange extract
Bakewell cake 76

Orange peel
Duck with cabbage, squash and pear 42

Panko breadcrumbs
Chorizo and Parmesan potato cakes 32
Wild boar with Scotch egg 80

Paprika
Sausage, chickpea, chorizo casserole 20

Parma ham
Wild boar with Scotch egg 80

Parsley
Fish soup 56
Mussels with cider, leek and bacon 64
Whole grilled sole with new potatoes 104
Mackerel tartare on toast with wasabi 136

Pastis
Fish soup 56

Pear
Duck with cabbage, squash and pear 42

Pea shoots
Parma ham-encrusted pork tenderloin 36

Peas
Summer stew with pan-seared cod 30
Parma ham-encrusted pork tenderloin 36
Pan-fried lamb loin chops 72

Pecans
Banana loaf 98

Pine nuts
Pan-roasted chicken supreme 110

Pomegranate
Gin-marinated venison 90

Pork
Parma ham-encrusted pork tenderloin 36
Crispy belly pork with apple juice jus 48

Port
Gin-marinated venison 90

Potatoes
Quick brunch 24
Summer stew with pan-seared cod 30
Chorizo and Parmesan potato cakes 32
Duck with cabbage, squash and pear 42
Crispy belly pork with apple juice jus 48
Fish soup 56
Pan-fried lamb loin chops 72
Ploughman's pasty 86
Gilthead bream on crushed potatoes 100
Whole grilled sole with new potatoes 104

Prawns
Fish soup 56

Puff pastry
Beetroot tarte tatin 124

Raspberries
Lemon meringue fudge cheesecake 58
Almond, mint and raspberry roulade 132

Real ale
Ale-steamed mussels 144

Red Cabbage
Duck with cabbage, squash and pear 42

Redcurrant jelly
Pan-fried lamb loin chops 72

Red peppers
Sausage, chickpea, chorizo casserole 20
Fish soup 56

Red wine
Sausage, chickpea, chorizo casserole 20
Duck with cabbage, squash and pear 42
Wild boar with Scotch egg 80
Slow-cooked lamb 114

Rocket
Sausage, chickpea, chorizo casserole 20

Rosemary
Sausage, chickpea, chorizo casserole 20
Wild boar with Scotch egg 80
Gin-marinated venison 90
Gilthead bream on crushed potatoes 100

Rouille
Fish soup 56

Saffron
Fish soup 56

Sage leaves
Pan-roasted chicken supreme 110

Salad leaves
Whole grilled sole with new potatoes 104
Smoked trout with baby leaf salad 140

Salmon
Fish soup 56

Samphire
Whole grilled sole with new potatoes 104
Ale-steamed mussels 144

Sausage meat
Wild boar with Scotch egg 80

Sausages
Sausage, chickpea, chorizo casserole 20
Quick brunch 24
Pork sausages with celeriac mash 118

Shallot
Gin-marinated venison 90
Whole grilled sole with new potatoes 104
Mackerel tartare on toast with wasabi 136
Smoked trout with baby leaf salad 140
Ale-steamed mussels 144

Spinach
Ploughman's pasty 86
Eggs Olivier 106

Spring onions
Chorizo and Parmesan potato cakes 32
Whole grilled sole with new potatoes 104
Slow-cooked lamb 114

Star anise
Parma ham-encrusted pork tenderloin 36
Duck with cabbage, squash and pear 42
Fish soup 56

Strawberries
Cream tea cheesecake 52

Strawberry jam
Cream tea cheesecake 52

Sweet potato
Wild boar with Scotch egg 80

Tarragon
Ale-steamed mussels 144

Thyme
Tomato ketchup 28
Duck with cabbage, squash and pear 42
Fish soup 56
Wild boar with Scotch egg 80
Gin-marinated venison 90
Pan-roasted chicken supreme 110
Beetroot tarte tatin 124

Tomatoes
Sausage, chickpea, chorizo casserole 20
Quick brunch 24
Tomato ketchup 28
Fish soup 56
Ploughman's pasty 86
Gilthead bream on crushed potatoes 100
Whole grilled sole with new potatoes 104
Smoked trout with baby leaf salad 140

Tomato purée
Sausage, chickpea, chorizo casserole 20
Fish soup 56
Wild boar with Scotch egg 80

Tonic water
Gin-cured sea trout 128

Trout
Gin-cured sea trout 128
Smoked trout with baby leaf salad 140

Venison
Gin-marinated venison 90

Wasabi
Mackerel tartare on toast with wasabi 136

Watercress
Gin-marinated venison 90
Eggs Olivier 106
Slow-cooked lamb 114
Beetroot tarte tatin 124
Smoked trout with baby leaf salad 140

White wine
Summer stew with pan-seared cod 30
Duck with cabbage, squash and pear 42
Fish soup 56
Pan-fried lamb loin chops 72

Wild boar
Wild boar with Scotch egg 80

Wild rocket
Gilthead bream on crushed potatoes 100

Worcestershire Sauce
Tomato ketchup 28

Yoghurt
Banana loaf 98
Smoked trout with baby leaf salad 140